Special Acknowledgements

Tiata Fahodzi thanks the major suppc
England for their continuing support.
Jenkins, Andrew Burton, Tim Welton ¡
Hoare, Nina Steiger, Rachel Taylor, Jo (
Jonathan Lloyd, Catherine Thornborro
and all at Soho Theatre; both organisa
making this production happen. Chery

G000141290

Tiata Fahodzi and the writer wish to thank **Adeboye Gbadebo**
for inspiring the formative paths for this production.

Production Acknowledgements

Sue Bird and Johanna Town at the Royal Court Theatre, Jacqui Beckford,
Steven Luckie, Dennis Charles, Akin Oguntusin and Olufunmilayo Ajana.

Tiata Fahodzi sent ULTZ and Moji Bamtefa to Nigeria to research the
production and buy materials for the costumes. They would like to
thank: Kunle Bamtefa for hosting the company, Latif Oloyede, Pastor
Wemimo Odunaiya and Olu Adeniregun for informing the set design;
Chief Dr T A Abiola-Oshodi, Rose Johnson and Alaka for help with the
costumes.

Tiata Fahodzi also remembers **YOMI A. MICHAEL** one of our
much loved actors and a Tiata Fahodzi alumnus. Yomi passed
away on the 7th March 2006 and will be greatly missed by us all.
His contribution to the profile of African Theatre in Britain, home
and abroad is immeasurable. May his soul rest in peace. Amen.

25 January 1965 – 7 March 2006

CAST

Ayo-Dele Ajana
(Abasina)

Ayo-Dele trained at Mountview Theatre School, in North London. Her theatre credits include The Gods are not to Blame, Tiata Delights 06 (Tiata Fahodzi); The Lion and the Jewel (Royal Court Theatre 50); My Kind Of Music (London Community Gospel Choir, UK tour); Rent (Prince of Wales & UK tour); White Folks (Tricycle Theatre). Other theatre credits include Hamlet, Twelfth Night (Birmingham Repertory Theatre, UK tour) and Leader of the Pack (Theatre Royal, Lincoln). TV: The Royal Variety Performance. Film: The Birthday Party and Salt Scrubbers (Best Actress BFM Short Film Awards 2004).

Kwaku Ankomah
(Soji)

Kwaku trained at RADA. His theatre credits include The Gods are not to Blame, Tiata Delights 06 (Tiata Fahodzi); Tamburlaine the Great (Rose Theatre, Southwark); Macbeth (Arcola Theatre/ Wiltons Music Hall, world tour); A Difference Between Friends (Paradoxos Theatre Company). Film and television includes: Batman Begins (Warner Brothers); Ultimate Force III (ITV); Cargo (Slate House Films).

Eddie Daniels (Pakimi)

Eddie trained at Richmond Drama School. Theatre credits include Tiata Delights 06 (Tiata Fahodzi); Critical Mass (Young Writers' Programme, Royal Court Theatre); Arabian Nights (Isleworth Actors' Company); Achidi J's Final Hour (Finborough); Ponies/Scotch and Water (Hen & Chickens).
TV: The Message (BBC Three).

Yvonne Dodoo
(Sola)

Since graduating from The Oxford School of Drama in 2004, Yvonne's credits include the inaugural Tiata Delights in 2004 and Tiata Delights 06 (Tiata Fahodzi), The Long Goodbye (Cockpit), Holby (BBC) and Waiting for Baba for the BBC World Service.

Nick Oshikanlu
(Afolabi)

Theatre includes: Tiata Delights 06 and The Gods are not to Blame (Tiata Fahodzi); My Home (London Bubble); Crocodile Seeking Refuge (Ice and Fire at Lyric Studios Hammersmith); National Alien Office (Riverside Studios); References to Salvador Dali Make Me Hot (Arcola Theatre, Young Vic Jerwood Award); Gompers (Arcola Theatre); What You Will (Globe Players); Once There Was, Once There Wasn't (Mirage Theatre Company); Cued Up (Half Moon Theatre Company); The Christmas Carol (Charles Cryer Theatre); Women Beware Women (aCCentuate Theatre Company at Landor Theatre). Television includes: Little Miss Jocelyn (Brown Eyed Boy Productions for BBC Three). Radio includes: Playing Away (BBC Radio); Preserved of God (Big Heart Media, BBC).

Richard Pepple
(Yinka)

Richard trained at Arts Educational School. His work in theatre includes: Tiata Delights 06 (Tiata Fahodzi); Daniel in The Sanctuary (Mile End Pavillion); Septimus Severus (reading) at Oval House. TV includes Nathan Barley (Channel 4); The Bill (ITV); Don't Shoot The Messenger (BBC).

TIATA FAHODZI

in co-production with The New Wolsey Theatre, Ipswich
and in association with Soho Theatre, London

present

THE ESTATE

by **Oladipo Agboluaje**

First performance at the New Wolsey Theatre, Ipswich
on Thursday 11 May 2006

followed by a national tour to

South Hill Park, Bracknell (18 – 19 May)
Contact, Manchester (31 May – 1 June)
Soho Theatre, London (6 – 17 June)

THE ESTATE

by Oladipo Agboluaje

Cast in order of appearance

Ekong **Wale Ojo**
Abasina **Ayo-Dele Ajana**
Afolabi **Nick Oshikanlu**
Pakimi **Eddie Daniels**
Helen **Ellen Thomas**
Soji **Kwaku Ankomah**
Sola **Yvonne Dodoo**
Samson **Wale Ojo**
Yinka **Richard Pepple**

Creative team

Director **Femi Elufowoju, jr**
Production Designer **ULTZ**
Costumes Consultant / Builder **Moji Bamtefa**
Lighting Designer **Trevor Wallace**
Composer **Akintayo Akinbode**
Sound Designer **Simon Deacon**
Casting **Nadine Hoare**
Dramaturg **Neil Grutchfield**
Assistants to the Director **Vernon Douglas, Rachel Briscoe**
Production Manager **David Duchin**
Deputy Stage Manager **Francesca Finney**
Assistant Stage Manager **Cleo Maynard**
Portraits **Stephen Cummiskey**
Publicity Design **Guray & Emel (artworkprint) and Jane Harper**

Ellen Thomas
(Helen)

In 2005 Ellen filmed Trial and Retribution (ITV); Casualty (BBC); The Marchioness Disaster (YTV); recorded Silver Street (BBC Radio Birmingham); Clare in the Community and features in Basic Instinct 2. Other credits are Tiata Delights 06 (Tiata Fahodzi); Blest Be the Tie (Royal Court); fourth and final series of Teachers (Channel 4); The Vagina Monologues (national tour); Twelfth Night (Royal Exchange Theatre); A Bitter Herb (Bristol Old Vic); Amen Corner (Tricycle/ Nottingham); Sisters (Channel 4 Sitcom Festival, Riverside Studios); Criminals in Love (Contact); Leonara's Dance (Black Theatre Co-operative); Moon on a Rainbow Shawl (Almeida Theatre); The American Clock and Fuente Ovejuna (both at the National Theatre); Echo in the Bone (The Women's Playhouse Trust at the Lyric Hammersmith); and Twelfth Night (Birmingham Rep). Other Television credits include Lenny Henry In Pieces and Lenny Henry Christmas Show (BBC); Holby City (BBC); The Bill (ITV); The Jury (Granada); Buried Treasure (LWT); William & Mary, Hidden City, Never Never (Channel 4); Active Defence (Granada); Where There's Smoke (Carlton); Ultraviolet (Channel 4); the regular character of Diane Simmons in London Bridge, Holding On (BBC); Kavannagh QC III, Ruth Rendell's Simisola, Beck (BBC); three series of Cardiac Arrest (BBC); The Lenny Henry Show (BBC); French & Saunders (BBC); Hallelujah Anyhow (BBC). Other Film credits include South West Nine; the award-winning Wonderland; Some Voices, Secret Laughter of Women and Breaking and Entering. Nominated Best Actress in: EMMA Awards 2003 & 2004, Screen Nation 2003 and Black Media Awards 2002.

Wale Ojo
(Ekong/Samson)

This is Wale's third production for Tiata Fahodzi and seventh with Femi Elufowoju, jr. He started his career as a child actor with Africa's first television station. His theatre credits include Tiata Delights 06; The Gods are not to Blame (Tiata Fahodzi); Bonded (Tiata Fahodzi; Oval House, UK Tour); The Big Men (G8 Season in the Olivier, RNT); Who Killed Mr Drum? (Riverside Studios); Widowers' House (Royal National Theatre); In The Talking Dark, Les Lancs (Royal Exchange, Manchester); Tickets & Ties (Theatre Royal, Stratford East); The Beatification of Area Boy (West Yorkshire Playhouse); Master Harold and The Boys (Bristol Old Vic); What The Butler Saw, Death and The Kings Horseman (Muson Centre, Lagos); King Baabu (Baxter Theatre, Cape Town/National Theatre Pretoria); Thieves Like Us, Acquisitive Case (Southwark Playhouse); Flamingo (The Gate Theatre); Rumplestiltskin (Nottingham Playhouse); Kaliyug (Contact Theatre, Manchester); N.B.N.I (Tricycle Theatre). Film credits include Cab Hustle (3K Films); Rage (Granite Filmworks); The Seer (Ladi Ladebo Productions); The Hard Case (Hellova Film Productions 2000); Six Demons (Naija Films). Television credits include The Bill (ITV); Heartburn Hotel, Grange Hill (BBC). Wale Ojo has also written several plays and has featured in numerous Radio productions for the BBC

CREATIVE TEAM

Oladipo Agboluaje (Writer)

Oladipo is a member of Soho Theatre's Writers Attachment Programme. Plays include Early Morning for Oval House and a version of Bertolt Brecht's Mother Courage and Her Children for the Eclipse Theatre Initiative, touring nationally in 2004. Recent work includes British-ish (New Wolsey Youth Theatre); For One Night Only (Pursued by a Bear); and Captain Britain (Talawa).

Akintayo Akinbode
(Music Composer)

Over the last twenty years Akintayo has composed and musically directed extensively around the country with productions including Tiata Fahodzi 2005 Summer production of The Gods are not to Blame (Arcola); Anthony & Cleopatra, Fen, Much Ado About Nothing, Peer Gynt, Great Expectations, Yerma and The Taming Of The Shrew (The Royal Exchange Theatre in Manchester). Others include: The Buddy Bolden Experience (Royal Exchange Studio and Edinburgh Festival); Ma Rainey's Black Bottom (Liverpool Playhouse); Weirdstone Of Brisingamen, Lysistrata, Generations Of The Dead and The Carver Chair (Contact Theatre); You Never Can Tell and Magnetic North (West Yorkshire Playhouse); Beauty and The Beast (New Vic, Stoke); Renegades, Totterdown Tanzi, Maid Marion and Her Merry Men (Bristol Old Vic); Charlotte's Web, Three Steps To Heaven, Blue Moon and Heart and Soul (Chester Gateway); Our Day Out, The Dispute, Storm (Generating Company) and Solomon and The Big Cat (Sheffield Crucible); Virtual Body, Flying Vets and Brooks Family Kitchen (Granada TV). Recent work includes: Heelz On Wheels 06 (Fittings); Voices (Upswing); A Whistle In The Dark (Royal Exchange Theatre); Cinderella (Liverpool Everyman); Horror For Wimps (Lips Service); Maritime Mysteries (Greenwich Docklands Festival). In addition to his theatre work he has also appeared as a presenter on the children's educational television programme Stop Look Listen, and has played in many bands including Chapter and The Verse, Distant Cousins and the almost legendary Walter And The Softies.

Moji Bamtefa (Costumes)

Storyteller, actor, costume builder and historian, Moji recently realised costumes for Tiata Fahodzi's production of The Gods are not to Blame at the Arcola, and Badejo Arts' Elemental Passions. Moji was theatre business manager for the Centre for Cultural Studies, University of Lagos where she worked extensively as a costume designer (and actor) for the National Troupe of Nigeria and the Lagos State Council for Arts and Culture. Her many credits include Saworoide (The Brassbells) by Mainframe Films, A Place called Home, The White Handkerchief and Twins of the Rain forest for South Africa M-Net. Moji runs IJAPA (ijapaokoyanrinbo@hotmail.com) a voluntary creative art organisation which encourages and aids young and disadvantaged people in discovering their innate talents and abilities.

Rachel Briscoe
(Assistant to the Director)

Directing credits include What Happened After Nora left Her Husband (reading – Arcola); The Lunatic, the Secret Sportsman and the Women Next Door by Stanley Eveling (Edinburgh Fringe); and The Flies (Cambridge St Chads Octagon). Assisting includes: The Baba Yaga (BAC); Twelfth Night (Cambridge Arts Theatre). Forthcoming projects include: directing the UK premiere of South African playwright Kobus Moolman's Full Circle (Oval House), and a devised project exploring the Correction method.

Simon Deacon (Sound Designer)

Simon gained a degree in Stage Management and Technical Theatre from Guildhall School of Music and Drama and since then has worked extensively in the entertainments industry specialising in sound and lighting. He has been part of the sound team at the New Wolsey on recent productions including Company, Robin Hood and the babes in the wood, The Good Companions and most recently Noel Coward's Private Lives. Simon was also the sound designer on The Wolsey's last rock 'n' roll panto Sleeping Beauty.

Vernon Douglas
(Assistant to the Director)

Since graduating from The Bristol Old Vic Theatre School in 1995, Vernon has worked as an actor for many leading companies in England including the National Theatre, Royal Exchange, Manchester, Contact Theatre, Citizens' Theatre, Glasgow, the Gate, Southwark Playhouse and Kultherset, Stockholm. His directing credits includes: The Fighter (St John's Church, Waterloo); Beloved (The Contact Theatre as part of the Live and Direct 4 programme). Vernon is currently assisting Sir Trevor Nunn on The Royal Hunt of the Sun at the National Theatre.

Femi Elufowoju, jr (Director)

Originally trained as a Solicitor in Nigeria and London, before obtaining a degree in Dramatic Arts from Bretton Hall, Leeds University. He subsequently worked as an actor for six years before retraining as a Regional Theatre Young Director in 1996 under Philip Hedley at Theatre Royal Stratford East. Femi founded Tiata Fahodzi in 1997 and has been its Artistic Director for the last nine years.

Other artistic associations include Associate Director (2004 traineeship) Royal Court Theatre London, Associate Director (2003)

West Yorkshire Playhouse, Leeds. Productions and readings directed for the Royal Court include Daydreams Of Hailey by Michael Bhim (Young Writers Festival, 2005); The Repast by Newton Moreno (International Writers, Summer Residency, 2005); Bone by John Donnelly (2004); Monkery by Apoorva Kale (International Writers, Summer Residency, 2004); Umze by Beartriz Goncalves (International Season, 2004); Senhora Of The Dunes by Egilberto Mendes (International Writers, Summer Residency, 2003). For the West Yorkshire Playhouse: Medea by Euripides, translated by Alistair Elliot; Off Camera by Marcia Layne. As guest director for Salisbury Playhouse: Dealer's Choice by Patrick Marber; as segment director for Queen's Golden Jubilee 50th Anniversary Celebrations: Commonwealth Parade (2002); as Guest Director for Theatre Royal, Stratford East/Swedish Tour; Tickets & Ties (devised); It's Good To Talk (devised). At Southwark Playhouse: Acquisitive Case by San Cassimally. Femi recently directed The Big Men by Richard Bean (2005) A Platform Performance in the Olivier Theatre as part of the Royal National Theatre's G8 Season of work.

Productions for Tiata Fahodzi include Tiata Delights 06 – a festival of play readings (Soho Theatre, London, 2006); The Gods are not to Blame by Ola Rotimi (Arcola Theatre, 2005); When Lightning Speaks by Debo Oluwatuminu (Soho Theatre, 2005); Tiata Delights a festival of play readings (Arcola Theatre, London, 2004); Sammy (devised, Theatre Royal, Stratford East & national tour, 2002); Abyssinia by Adewale Ajadi (Southwark Playhouse & national tour, 2001); Makinde by Femi Elufowoju, jr (Oval House & national tour, 2000); Bonded by Sesan Ogunledun (Oval House & national tour, 1999); Booked! (devised, Oval House & national tour, 1998).

Neil Grutchfield (Dramaturg)

Neil Grutchfield read Drama and Theatre Studies at Royal Holloway, University of London before joining the Box Office at the Royal Court Theatre in 1993. Neil has been a part of the Royal Court ever since. As well as his current position of Sales Manager he has supported the YWP writers group, worked as a Front of House Manager and organized script meetings between the Literary Department and the Box Office. Neil's interest in new writing has lead to him becoming a freelance script reader and he has been employed by the Theatre Writing Partnership, the Eclipse Programme, Nottingham Playhouse, Sonia Friedman Productions, Ambassadors Theatre Group and Zenith Productions readings plays, screenplays, treatments and outlines. In recent years Neil took part in script selection for the Eclipse Laboratory – a programme based in the East Midlands aimed at developing the work of new black British writers. Neil also assisted the workshop leader in running the Momentum Young Writers Programme at the Royal and Derngate Theatres from 2004-2005 culminating in work being performed at the Momentum Festival in Summer 2005. Neil is now a freelance Dramaturg and has worked with Tiata Fahodzi, developing Dipo Agboluaje's The Estate. He is currently working with Segun Lee-French on a project with Big Creative Ideas.

ULTZ (Production Designer)

ULTZ was Production Designer for The Gods Are Not To Blame produced by Tiata Fahodzi and directed by Femi Elufowoju, jr at the Arcola Theatre last year. In the West End he designed When Harry Met Sally starring Luke Perry and Alyson Hannigan, Me And Mamie O'rourke starring French and Saunders, A Madhouse In Goa starring Vanessa Redgrave; for the RSC, 16 productions including The Twin-Rivals (Olivier Award Nomination – Best Designer), Good (London & Broadway) and The Art Of Success (RSC & Manhattan Theatre Club); for the Royal Court, 11 world premieres including this season's The Winterling directed by Ian Rickson, Femi Elufowoju, jr's production of Bone, Fallout (Evening Standard Theatre Awards Nomination – Best Design) and the award-winning Mojo (Royal Court, West End & Steppenwolf Theater Company, Chicago). Other designs include: The Harder They Come (Theatre Royal Stratford East); Arturo Ui, The Ramayana (National Theatre Olivier Stage); Tanika Gupta's adaptation of Hobson's Choice (Evening Standard Theatre Awards Nomination – Best Design, Young Vic & National Tour); Der Ferne Klang (Opera North); As You Like It (Stockholms Stadsteater); Julius Caesar, The Cherry Orchard (Stratford, Ontario); A

Walk In The Woods (Edmonton, Alberta); Twelfth Night (Ginza Saison Tokyo); for Bayerische Staatsoper in Munich: Xerxes (OpernWelt Critics' Award – Best Design); La Clemenza Di Tito, The Rake's Progress, Die Entfuhrung Aus Dem Serail. ULTZ directed: the musical Summer Holiday starring Darren Day (premiere at Blackpool Opera House/National Tour/London Apollo/South African Tour); Da Boyz – a hip hop version of 'The Boys from Syracuse' which ULTZ devised with DJ Excalibah & MC Skolla; Niraj Chag's musical Baiju Bawra, The Taming Of The Shrew – The Women's Version; and the British premiere of Lorca's The Public (Theatre Royal Stratford East); The Boyfriend, What The Butler Saw (Nottingham Playhouse); Noises Off (Leicester Haymarket); Jesus Christ Superstar (in Danish at Aarhus & Cophenhagen); Don Giovanni and Cosi Fan Tutte (in Japanese at the Tokyo Globe); L'Elisir D'Amore (Tiroler Landestheater, Austria); Die Fledermaus (Bavaria); Pericles (London & Stockholms Stadsteater); A Midsummer Night's Dream (National Arts Centre, Ottawa); Dragon (National Theatre); 4 plays by Jean Genet – The Maids and Deathwatch (RSC); The Screens (California); The Blacks (Market Theatre Johannesburg/ Grahamstown Festival/Stockholms Stadsteater).

Trevor Wallace (Lighting Designer)

Recent lighting designs include: The Gods are not to Blame (Tiata Fahodzi at the Arcola Theatre); Notes on Falling Leaves, Bone, Fresh Kills, and A Day in Dull Armour (Royal Court). Other lighting designs: Golden Boy, Nobody's Perfect, Kit and the Widow – The Fat Lady Sings (Yvonne Arnaud Theatre, Guildford); Cabaret and Sweet Charity (Electric Theatre, Guildford); The Weir (Theatro Technis); Closer (Barn Theatre); Into the Woods, The Changeling (Sandpit Theatre, St Albans); The School of Night (Shattered Windscreen); Comedy of Errors, Grimm Tales, Richard III, Cyrano de Bergerac, Les Enfants du Paradis and A Midsummer Night's Dream (Minack Theatre, Cornwall). Film work includes: Director of Photography for Glyn Maxwell's The Best Man (Felix Films), directed by John Croker.

The Estate in rehearsal

Ayo-Dele Ajana

Wale Ojo

Kwaku Ankomah

Richard Pepple and Yvonne Dodoo

Ellen Thomas

Femi Elufowoju, jr

Photographs © Stephen Cummiskey

TIATA FAHODZI

The words 'Tiata Fahodzi' are an amalgamation of Yoruba (Nigeria) and Twi (Ghana) which translate as 'theatre of the emancipated'.

Founded in 1997 by the company's current Artistic Director, Femi Elufowoju, jr, the company remains Britain's only African touring theatre company.

Essentially, Tiata Fahodzi demonstrates the cultural experience of Africans in Britain through mainstream theatre. The company explores the richness and heritage of theatre sourced from people living within the British African communities encompassing Education, New Writing and Theatre Productions which is its main artistic drive. The company produces new work through commissions, it revives theatre from the classical canon, advocates education initiatives by working in partnerships with skilled organisation and individuals specialised in young peoples theatre and we create opportunities for aspiring and emerging British African theatre practitioners.

Our work albeit targeted towards a specific critical cultural mass (Africans living in Britain) attracts an all inclusive British audience.

'There has not been a better time to see Tiata Fahodzi'
Time Out Magazine on Tiata Fahodzi's 2005 production of Ola Rotimi's *The Gods are not to Blame*

Mo Sesay as Odewale. Photo by Stephen Cummiskey.

Tiata Fahodzi Team

Artistic Director **Femi Elufowoju, jr**
Executive Director **Susan Marnell**
Education Associate **Steven Downs**
Board: **Janice Acquah** (Chair), **Jacqueline Awidi, Fiona Burtt, Adeboye Gbadebo, Archibald R.H Graham, Fiona Sax Ledger, Jenny Worton**

Contacting the Theatre

Tiata Fahodzi
AH112 Aberdeen Centre
22-24 Highbury Grove
London N5 2EA
Tel/Fax 020 7226 3800
Email: info@tiatafahodzi.com
Website: www.tiatafahodzi.com

Productions 1998–2006:

Booked (1998) Oval House, Tabernacle London, devised by Freddie Annobil-Dodoo, Angela Appiah, Femi Elufowoju jr, Tunde Euba, Josephine Inoniyegha, Usifu Jalloh and Mary Njojo Nduta.

Bonded (1999) National Tour, written by Sesan Ogunledun

Makinde (2000) National Tour, written by Femi Elufowoju, jr

Abyssinia (2001) National Tour, written by Adewale Ajadi

Sammy (2002) National Tour, written by Femi Elufowoju, jr

Steppin Out (2003) Deighton Centre, Huddersfield, written by Angie Smith

Tiata Delights (2004) Festival of New Writing, Arcola Theatre London; Writers: Dipo Agboluaje, Tunde Euba, Amma Duodu, Harold Kimmel, Reginald Ofodile and Debo Oluwatuminu

It Takes A Whole Village (2004) Lawrence Batley Theatre, Huddersfield, written by Audrey Henry-Quarcoo and Mycil Muhammed

Appointment At Diamoniques (2004) Lawrence Batley Theatre, Huddersfield, written by Mel Mills

When Lightning Speaks...Home (2005) Open House Season, Soho Theatre London, written by Debo Oluwatuminu

The Gods Are Not To Blame (2005) Arcola Theatre London, written by Ola Rotimi

Tiata Delights 06 (2006) Festival of New Writing, Soho Theatre London; Writers: Oladipo Agboluaje, Kofi Agyemang, Michael Bhim, San Cassimally, Segun Lee-French and Valerie Mason-John

COMING SOON

Forthcoming work includes Creation 2 Production **(Summer 2006)**, an education initiative in association with South Hill Park, Bracknell (working in secondary schools in the Berkshire county on writing/performance skills for the theatre).
Also Productions with Quicksilver Theatre (2007), Ipswich's Eastern Angles (2008), and Unicorn Theatre (2009).

ROY WILLIAMS, 2007

Autumn 2007 will also see Tiata Fahodzi touring a new **Roy Williams play** in a major co-production, **working title 'Finding Joe'** The production concludes the final part in the trilogy of plays (*Lift Off* and *Clubland* both written by Roy and originally produced by the Royal Court). This commissioned play explores the perils and trappings of misplaced loyalty and fame as seen through the eyes of a second generation Ghanaian based in Britain. The play also focuses on the historical rift between Caribbean and West Africans co-existing in Britain.

New Wolsey Theatre, Ipswich
(Co-Producers)

The New Wolsey Ipswich is a vibrant theatre in the heart of Suffolk's county town. We produce, co-produce and host an eclectic mix of events that are accessible, diverse and of the highest possible quality. The New Wolsey won the TMA/Arts Council England Eclipse Award in 2003 for its work in tackling racism in theatre and for audience development. We have strong links with our local communities through our extensive outreach and education programmes.

Along with Birmingham Rep and Nottingham Playhouse, we are co-producers of Eclipse Theatre. In 2004 we co-produced James Baldwin's landmark play *Blues for Mr Charlie* with Talawa Theatre Company and last year we extended our relationship with Talawa by co-producing an educational tour, *Captain Britain*, which explored issues surrounding self-image and multiculturalism in contemporary Britain. *Captain Britain*, like *The Estate*, was written by Oladipo Agboluaje, our Writer-in-Residence last year.

We are delighted to be co-producing *The Estate* with Tiata Fahodzi and in association with Soho Theatre.

For a constantly updated view of our activities visit www.wolseytheatre.co.uk

Soho Theatre

Soho Theatre is passionate in its commitment to new writing, producing a year-round programme of bold, original and accessible new plays – many of them from first-time playwrights.

'a foundry for new talent…one of the country's leading producers of new writing' Evening Standard

Soho Theatre offers an invaluable resource to emerging playwrights. Our training and outreach programme includes the innovative Under 11s scheme, the Young Writers' Group (18-25s) and a burgeoning series of Nuts and Bolts writing workshops designed to equip new writers with the basic tools of playwriting. We offer the nation's only unsolicited script-reading service, reporting on over 2,000 plays per year. We aim to develop and showcase the most promising new work through the national Verity Bargate Award, the Launch Pad scheme and the Writers' Attachment Programme, working to develop writers not just in theatre but also for TV and film.

'a creative hotbed… not only the making of theatre but the cradle for new screenplay and television scripts' The Times

Contemporary, comfortable, air-conditioned and accessible, Soho Theatre is busy from early morning to late at night. Alongside the production of new plays, it is also an intimate venue to see leading national and international comedians in an eclectic programme mixing emerging new talent with established names.

'London's coolest theatre by a mile' Midweek

Soho Theatre, 21 Dean St, London W1D 3NE
Admin: 020 7287 5060
Box Office: 0870 429 6883
Minicom: 020 7478 0148
www.sohotheatre.com

Email information list
For regular programme updates and offers, join our free email list by visiting
www.sohotheatre.com

ACTING • MUSICAL THEATR
CLASSICAL ACTING • SCREEN &
RADIO PERFORMANCE • THEATR
DIRECTING • TECHNICAL THEATR
• ACTING • MUSICAL THEATRE
CLASSICAL ACTING • MUSICA
THEATRE • CLASSICAL ACTIN
SCREEN & RADIO PERFORMANC
THEATRE DIRECTIN
TECHNICAL THEATR
ACTING • MUSICAL TH
CLASSICAL ACTING •
MUSICAL THEATRE • CL
ACTING • SCREEN • RADIO

MOUNTVIEW
ACADEMY OF THEATRE ARTS

offers undergraduate and
postgraduate courses in Acting,
Musical Theatre and Techncial Theatre

Validated by the University of East Anglia
Accredited by the National Council for Drama Training

www.mountview.ac.uk
Tel: 020 8881 2201

Mountview is committed to equal opportunities

Oval House Southern Africa Season presents Full Frontal Theatre's

QABUKA
Adventures in exile

Devised by the company. Conceived and Directed by Ben Evans.

Oval house

Imagine seeing snow for the first time

Imagine laughing so hard you wet the seat

Imagine fleeing from a government you'd elected

Imagine a love affair with your Oyster Card

Imagine what it's like to die in a foreign country

Imagine finding peace

Devised and improvised from the personal stories of over one hundred Zimbabweans-in-exile, Full Frontal Theatre presents a magical and exuberant look at the lives of Zimbabweans living in the UK.

A postcard from the edge which deftly finds the humour in tragedy and the mischief in tribulation.

"An outstanding piece of theatre" The Zimbabwean

£12 / £6 concessions (including Refugee Community Organisations)
BOX OFFICE 020 7582 7680
Book on-line **WWW.OVALHOUSE.COM** (no fee)

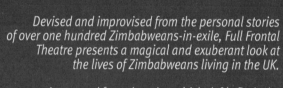

28th June–15th July (Tues-Sat)
7:45pm (except Saturdays 1st & 8th 6pm)
Preview Wednesday 28th June: all tickets £6
Saturdays 1st & 8th July 6pm (World Cup friendly!)
Signed performances Wednesday 5th & Saturday 8th July
Post show discussion Wednesday 5th July
Tuesday 4th July: Patson Muzuwa, chair of the Zimbabwe Association will lead a debate on the political future of Zimbabwe.

ARTS COUNCIL ENGLAND

MERIDIAN THEATRE COMPANY   interact   **OVAL HOUSE THEATRE,** 52-54 Kennington Oval, London SE11

Supported by Interact, in association with Meridian Theatre Company; by the Unity Theatre Trust; and the Rausing Abrahams Arts Fund.

It is not often that Tiata Fahodzi discovers a new play that is packed with characters that are larger than life, sharp universal humour and vibrant theatricality.

Oladipo's Agboluaje's *The Estate* is a hoot, and I look forward to sharing the pleasures this production has given me as its director with all who encounter this slice of contemporary Nigeria, opened up in all its glory on the British stage.

Femi Elufowoju, jr
May 2006

Oladipo Agboluaje
THE ESTATE

OBERON BOOKS
LONDON

First published in 2006 by Oberon Books Ltd
521 Caledonian Road, London N7 9RH
Tel: 020 7607 3637 / Fax: 020 7607 3629
e-mail: info@oberonbooks.com
www.oberonbooks.com

A catalogue record for this book is available from the British
Library.

ISBN: 1 84002 653 7

Cover photograph by Stephen Cummiskey

Printed in Great Britain by Antony Rowe Ltd, Chippenham.

dedicated to
'Niyi and Iyabode

For all your support, love and kindness

Neil Grutchfield, Susan Marnell,
Jonathan Lloyd, Nina Steiger, Rachel Taylor,
Rose Sirico-Codling, Peter Rowe, Cheryl Martin,
Kwadwo Osei-Nyame jr, Steven Luckie, Jana Manekshaw,
Mr and Mrs D B Smith, Pat Waller, Ndubuisi Anike,
Akin Oladimeji, Al Celestine, Jayeola Maclean,
Nasika Pace, Anthony and Caroline Costello, Peter Wilson,
'Wale and Titi Agboluaje

CHARACTERS

HELEN ADEYEMI
late Chief Adeyemi's wife, mother of Sola

YINKA ADEYEMI
eldest son of Chief Adeyemi

SOJI ADEYEMI
Yinka's junior brother

SOLA ADEYEMI
Helen's daughter, half-sister of Yinka and Soji

PASTOR LOMI PAKIMI

ABASINA
house-girl

SAMSON
Abasina's elder brother

EKONG
the Adeyemis' driver

AFOLABI
the Adeyemis' caretaker

All the action takes place in the
sitting-room of the Adeyemi mansion.

THE WAKE

Early morning. The sitting-room of the Adeyemi mansion. It is in a state of upheaval. Offstage-right is the front door. The kitchen door is behind the sitting-room. Stage-left, the staircase leading up to the landing and the bedrooms. 1980s ostentation drips from everywhere – except for the chandelier, which is missing a few bulbs. There is a crude vase on the cabinet, which is incongruous with the opulent surroundings. Chief Adeyemi's portrait hangs on the wall. He wears a full Yoruba outfit. Two smaller portraits hang on either side. One is of Chief Adeyemi with his first wife and their two sons, Yinka and Soji. The other is of Chief Adeyemi with his second wife, Helen, and their daughter, Sola. AFOLABI and EKONG rush in and out of the kitchen with crates of drinks. ABASINA drags along a heavy bag of rice. HELEN is on the phone:

HELEN: If you're double-booked, *nko*? That is my problem? Look! The food arrives *on time* or no payment! (*Slams down the receiver.*) Idiot. (*Clocks ABASINA.*) Look at this lowlife. Because I allowed you to pass through the sitting-room.

ABASINA lifts the bag. AFOLABI enters from kitchen. Helps ABASINA.

Ah, Mr Afolabi. You've finished off-loading the drinks?

AFOLABI exits front door. ABASINA exits kitchen. HELEN sits on the sofa. Beside her, her head-tie and handbag. Samples of fabric litter the sofa, central table and floor. HELEN takes a pair of scissors off the sofa and puts them on the central table. Copies of 'Ovation' lie on the central table. HELEN flicks through each magazine, checking that none of the fabrics worn in the photos match the samples. ABASINA enters from front door with a crate of drinks. HELEN snaps her fingers. ABASINA puts down the crate and stands beside HELEN.

Let me see that one...*that one*! (*The sample is next to her.*) Abasina, you are blind?

ABASINA: (*Picks up the sample.*) Sorry, Ma. (*Treads on a sample on the floor.*)

HELEN: Get your charcoal feet off my material!

ABASINA: Sorry, Ma. (*Curtseys as she hands the sample to HELEN.*)

HELEN: You are a good for nothing. If not that Papa pitied your cursed family, I should have flung you back into the bush… Animal. (*Snatches the sample from her, flings another sample at her.*) Tell the designer: this one is for the wake. (*Gives ABASINA another sample.*) For the funeral. (*Another sample.*) For the first half of the party. (*Another sample.*) For the second half. (*Another sample.*) For the Thanksgiving. I want them ready by this evening.

ABASINA waits. EKONG passes into kitchen. AFOLABI exits through front door.

Ehen?

ABASINA: Mr Ekong never finish.

HELEN: What is your business with Ekong? (*Claps her hand in disgust.*) Can your father afford a driver? Mind yourself. *Mind yourself*! Get out!

ABASINA curtseys and exits through kitchen

Let me find a speck of dust on them, you will see.

HELEN heads for the stairs. EKONG enters from kitchen.

EKONG: Eh, Madam, Alhaji say 'no money, no diesel'.

HELEN: And it is just now you're telling me?

EKONG: Madam, you say I should bring the drinks inside –

HELEN: You told Alhaji that *I* say I will pay him later?

EKONG: I tell am, Madam. He say you never pay am for the last diesel –

HELEN: (*Puts on her head-tie, grabs her handbag.*) I have to do everything myself. (*Her mobile phone rings.*) Sola … What are you still doing on campus? … No, no! Start coming now… Ekong is busy… Charter taxi! Hold on. (*Snaps her fingers at EKONG.*) Get the car ready. (*As EKONG exits.*) Fool.

HELEN exits through front door, continuing her conversation with SOLA.

Is that not Wale's voice? Ask him to bring you home now…

Enter SOJI, sweating profusely. He is dressed in a short-sleeved shirt, jeans and sandals. AFOLABI carries his bags.

AFOLABI: Everything is rush-rush! (*Puts down the bags.*)

SOJI: That shouldn't stop her from saying hello properly.

AFOLABI: She go to buy diesel for the generator. You know Power Holdings is always withholding power. They change their name from NEPA, still is the same no light –

SOJI: (*Looks around.*) Bloody…! Nothing is ready.

AFOLABI: Is the labour strike is causing all sorts of delay. And also, fear did not allow us to go out on weekend. See soldier and police bruuu! bruuu! (*Gesticulates shooting.*)

SOJI: At each other?

AFOLABI: They want to collect bribe from the same person. Twenty civilian die from stray bullet. Ehn, person leave his house to follow his own business –

SOJI: Yes, yes, yes…

AFOLABI: Ah-ha. Is only yesterday we buy the cow. Caterer has not deliver the *oyinbo* food. Ekong queue for three days at petrol station.

SOJI: So? She couldn't send Sule or Edward to the airport? Or are they queuing for petrol too?

AFOLABI: You don't know? They sack them.

SOJI: At a time like this? What was she thinking –

AFOLABI: Is Pastor tell Madam to sack them… But I am happy to see your face. You don't even ask of me on your last visit. Is Papa not tell you I am in the hospital?

SOJI: No time.

AFOLABI: Is okay. As you are big professor, Nigeria's problem is on your mind. You remember when you are student you are saying you will help us poor people. The English that Wole Soyinka cannot understand, you will talk it and save our country. My children, I have to help them. I suppose to retire since but life is too tough –

SOJI: It's tough for all of us…

AFOLABI: Ah-ha. You remember when you are small child. I drive you in wheelbarrow. I carry you on my back. You are laughing, calling my name: 'Afolabi, do it again! Afolabi, carry me again!' Of all Papa children, you are the one who treat me well. Just like Papa. That's why nobody else in my life I work for. As Papa do me, I know his children will do me well, too.

SOJI puts his hand in his pocket. AFOLABI waits expectantly. SOJI brings out a handkerchief and wipes his face.

SOJI: Oh. I don't have naira on me.

AFOLABI: Even poor man like me, I know how to spend pounds… Is okay. I am around…

Enter SOLA from front door. AFOLABI runs to collect her bag.

Little sister, welcome!

SOLA: Thank you, Baba. (*Gives him money.*)

AFOLABI: God will replenish your pocket! (*Looks behind her.*) Ah, is that not Uncle Wale –

SOLA: The canopy is here.

AFOLABI: Ah-ha! Please help me tell Pastor the canopy has arrive. (*Bows as he exits.*)

SOLA: Hi.

SOJI: Hi. How are you?

SOLA: Fine.

SOJI: And your studies?

SOLA: Fine. So. You got your full-time appointment.

SOJI: Uh-huh. You…you look good.

SOLA: London is doing you favours.

SOJI: When it wants to.

SOLA: When did you land?

SOJI: A few minutes ago. And you?

SOLA: Just now.

SOJI: Of course, of course… Um, yeah, um, good to see you.

SOLA: Good. You too. You didn't keep in touch.

SOJI: *You* never kept in touch.

SOLA: You were supposed to send your new email address.

SOJI does a phone gesture.

You should have called. Then I remembered; it's Soji. You leave everything to chance.

SOJI: I know what I want.

SOLA: Uh-huh. (*Waits, expectantly. Picks up her bag and heads for the stairs.*)

SOJI: Sola…

SOLA turns around to face him.

I'll sort everything out. Trust me –

Enter PASTOR LOMI PAKIMI from upstairs. He is on his mobile phone.

PAKIMI: What inflation? Am I the Minister of Finance? You deliver the chickens at our agreed price or I go elsewhere! … Better. No African time! (*Hangs up.*) What a delight! Brother and sister together! Dr Adeyemi, welcome. The Lord answers our prayer for your safe arrival. (*They shake hands.*)

SOJI: Yinka isn't here yet.

PAKIMI: Living amongst unbelievers makes our brother cynical. Brother Yinka will arrive safe and sound, in Jesus' name… *In Jesus' name.*

SOLA: Amen.

PAKIMI: You are fine, my daughter?

SOLA: Yes, Pastor Pakimi, thank you.

PAKIMI: Architect to be! That will be added to another coveted title. If you know how many of our young church-men wish to confer on you the honour of Mrs, your head will swell like overripe paw-paw. I can picture it: the society event of the century. It will be just like the Royal Wedding.

SOJI: And we all know how that ended.

PAKIMI: Brother Soji, don't wish ill for your sister.

SOLA: I want to complete my studies.

PAKIMI: Yes but you must meet a suitable partner now.

SOLA: I want to be independent first.

PAKIMI: But you need a man, your other half, to complete you. More so for you, Brother Soji. I keep saying it. My London branch overflows with good Christian girls.

SOJI: Yeah. Pastor Michael jokes that he can smell the estrogen during the singles programme.

PAKIMI: In time our heavenly Father will cleanse Pastor Michael of his vulgarity.

SOJI: I'd better pop into his service before the Lord washes out his mouth.

PAKIMI: You will come out of God's house with something greater.

SOJI: Fela will be playing on my iPod.

PAKIMI: The choir will drown out that idol worshipper's pagan music.

SOJI: Doesn't it bother you, referring to our traditional beliefs as pagan?

PAKIMI: Some things are beyond human understanding.

SOJI: Such as why we denigrate our own beliefs –

PAKIMI: The caterer must have arrived by now.

SOLA: Mother has a list of things for me to do. Pastor… (*Exits upstairs.*)

PAKIMI: My daughter… Brother Soji, I've not even proffered my condolences. Your father was a rarity: an honest businessman. Like Abraham, Papa was obedient to God's every wish. And like Abraham, God blessed him with abundance and with you wonderful children. You will say you don't believe in prayers. But we pray for you constantly that your academic career blossoms. That you remain a worthy son of Papa.

SOJI: Um, thank you.

PAKIMI: And so a fitting, trouble-free send-off is the only compensation we mortals can honour Papa with. My ultra-modern Church is fully prepared. I hope every other arrangement is to your satisfaction.

SOJI: (*Looks around at the mess.*) Um, ye-ah…

PAKIMI: Papa was my Godsend. Who could have imagined me becoming the leader of Nigeria's biggest Church. If Sule had not taken ill I would not have driven Papa to his business lunch with the Lord's anointed, Reverend Billy Robertson. This house, I will always be part of. So please let us make things go smoothly.

HELEN enters through front door. ABASINA enters through kitchen and waits to be noticed

HELEN: (*Off.*) When you put the canopy on the driveway how will our guests enter? Or what kind of idiots are you? (*Inside.*) Pastor, I asked you to supervise these people now.

PAKIMI: (*Testily.*) I told Afolabi to tell me when the canopy arrives. (*Exits.*)

SOJI: Oh, yeah. He told Sola to…

HELEN: Brother Soji, welcome. Sorry I couldn't stop. Those lazy labour union people, they are causing us all kind of problem.

SOJI: I thought we were getting a marquee. Papa would have wanted a marquee.

HELEN: We were late in hiring it. The Odibos and the Jimohs, they too are having parties today. The canopies are made in London. They are to Papa's taste.

SOJI: Where is Ekong?

HELEN: He's been busy all day... Sola is here?

SOJI: Upstairs. Will Ekong be too busy to pick Yinka from the airport?

HELEN: If there is work to do.

SOJI: Oh, okay. I'll be here to see that.

HELEN: But you can see for yourself... (*Notices ABASINA.*) What is it?

ABASINA: The designer say the cloth go ready by this afternoon. Welcome, Sah–

HELEN: Take Brother's bags upstairs then join the aunties in the backyard to prepare the rice.

ABASINA curtseys and exits upstairs with SOJI's bags.

SOJI: I thought we'd already sorted out the clothes.

HELEN: The material we decided on; the Oloidi's wore one for their son's birthday. The Inyangs wore another for their child-naming –

SOJI: You've gone for a whole new batch?

HELEN: We cannot wear cast-offs for your father's funeral. When people see our photographs in 'Ovation', you want them to mock us? People must know that we remain a family to reckon with.

SOJI: Tell me at least Yinka knows.

HELEN: Not yet. (*Hopefully.*) You will talk to him for us.

SOLA enters from stairs.

(*To SOLA.*) Mama Buky says the pastries are ready.

SOLA: Good morning, mother.

HELEN: Ekong!

SOLA: I said good morning.

HELEN: Morning, morning! *Oya*, there's no time to waste.

ABASINA enters from upstairs. Exits through kitchen as EKONG enters from kitchen.

SOLA: (*To EKONG.*) I will drop by my friend's –

HELEN: (*To EKONG.*) Join Afolabi and cut the grass behind the shed.

EKONG hands over the keys to SOLA. He hesitates.

What?

EKONG: Madam I never chop breakfast.

HELEN eyes EKONG. EKONG exits sheepishly.

HELEN: (*To SOLA.*) Ekong is busy. You can drive yourself.

SOJI: I'll drive you there.

HELEN: And don't stop at any friend's house! The wake…

SOJI eyes HELEN.

It's Sola. It's Sola I'm talking to.

SOLA exits. SOJI follows. HELEN stops him.

Eh, Brother Soji… It will help if you support me. Papa wanted all of us to be close. I shouldn't remind you of that.

SOJI: Right… You can start by telling Yinka yourself, then.

HELEN: Yes. When he arrives… Look, sorry about Ekong. Honest drivers, you can't find them. Leave anything in the car they will steal it. That's why we sacked the other drivers. Ekong too is a first-class criminal. We are just managing him. I should have come to pick you myself. Sorry my brother. My big brother.

SOJI: Yeah, yeah…

HELEN: This inconvenience, it is all for Papa. And you know what Papa wants…

SOJI: Papa gets. And what Papa wants…

HELEN: Is only the best. I'm glad you understand.

SOJI: Yeah… Your money-changer is near Mama Buky's?

HELEN: (*Searches her bag. Hands SOJI a business card.*) You are learning. Dashing your money to the banks when the black market offers a better rate.

SOJI: I was doing Nigeria a favour.

HELEN: Doing Nigeria a favour? Dr Adeyemi! (*Laughs uncontrollably.*)

SOLA: (*Off. Angrily.*) Are you coming?

PAKIMI enters from front door.

SOJI: Pastor Pakimi. (*Exits.*)

PAKIMI: I see we are in good humour. Do we have time for your morning prayers?

HELEN: There is always time for God in this house. (*They exit upstairs.*)

ABASINA enters from kitchen. She looks at Chief Adeyemi's portrait and pats her stomach. She sighs. A noise from the kitchen. ABASINA tidies up the sitting-room. EKONG enters wearily from kitchen with a container of food. He holds it up, making a sign of thanks to ABASINA and collapses onto the sofa.

ABASINA: Mr Ekong, no let Madam see you for sitting-room.

EKONG: Is only shout she will shout. Because Papa die, then we should follow him to him grave? Where you go before?

ABASINA: I dey for backyard. See the time. When you go go collect Uncle Yinka?

EKONG: (*Sighs.*) Tell Madam I am going to airport. Work no dey finish for this house.

ABASINA: Is work we are here to work.

EKONG: I am driver, not gardener. You never hear of division of labour? We suppose to join the Labour people strike.

ABASINA: Mr Ekong, no start that one again.

EKONG: I beg, don't talk like Afolabi. Upon all his loyalty what is his reward? Abasina, I always tell you: you have no future with these people. Nothing you can get from dem.

ABASINA: Make I follow you return to village? That one is not my future.

EKONG: Why not? We will support ourselves instead of doing slave to rich people.

ABASINA: Everyday you dey talk this kind of talk. But everyday you return to work.

EKONG: Soon.

ABASINA: 'Soon.' Since how long you dey sing your revolution song? Mr Ekong, this life is matter of money. And na here money dey.

EKONG: And where the money come from? Oil pipeline is running through my backyard for village. But our people, all of us we are housemaid and driver in Lagos. When is people like your brother Samson dey carry you and your people come to do slave for here.

ABASINA: Because nothing dey for village –

EKONG: So, is not you I hear abusing Samson? Is not you telling him that you don't come to Lagos to do house-girl?

ABASINA: Mr Ekong, that is between me and my brother. Opportunity is here. When the chance come, I will take it. That is how Nigeria is. That is how we have to live.

EKONG: How things will change when poor person like you is thinking like this?

ABASINA: So what are we poor people suppose to do? Make we secede from Nigeria?

EKONG: Why not? Hausa man have secede already.

ABASINA: *Mr Ekong*! Where you hear dat one?

EKONG: Hausa man do Sharia law for their state, which is unconstitutional. Dat one no be secede? The thing wey dem

31

no let Igbo man do. Fela talk am. Our people, we fear too much. Even when we have to look after ourself.

ABASINA: I fit look after myself. I know wetin I dey do.

EKONG: I hope so. But I know say, one day-one day, things go change for this country. When that time come, hey, I will line up Madam, all the rich people, politicians, army generals – (*Makes a firing squad gesture.*)

The front door opens. EKONG snatches the container and dashes into kitchen. ABASINA cleans hurriedly. AFOLABI enters and stands by the entrance.

ABASINA: (*Laughs.*) Baba, na you…

AFOLABI: Is Ekong I'm looking for.

ABASINA: He don carry the food go meet you for outside.

AFOLABI: He don't know that hunger is killing person? Madam will soon come down now, ah! (*Heads for front door.*)

ABASINA: Baba… (*Gestures to him to pass through to the kitchen.*)

AFOLABI: Is all right, my daughter.

ABASINA: By the time you reach backyard, Ekong go finish the food…

AFOLABI hesitates. He is half-way through the sitting-room when HELEN and PAKIMI enter from upstairs.

HELEN: Papa never wasted money on anything homemade, so check them well. Those crafty wholesalers, they pack the local napkins inside foreign cartons…

PAKIMI: I say don't worry, ah! This dealer is my church member… Ah, Afolabi, any problem?

AFOLABI: No, Sah.

PAKIMI: No? How long have you been working here? That it is now in your twilight years that you decide to set a bad example to the other staff. Because Papa is no longer with us, *abi*?

AFOLABI: Sorry, Sah. (*Makes to exit through front door.*)

PAKIMI: Ah-ah. Afolabi…

AFOLABI realises his mistake, bows apologetically and exits through kitchen.

HELEN: Remember his age, oh… (*To ABASINA.*) The clothes are ready.

ABASINA: Yes, Ma.

PAKIMI: It's on my way. I'll drop you there. (*Exits through front door.*)

ABASINA follows PAKIMI. HELEN eyes her. She exits through kitchen. HELEN looks fondly at Chief Adeyemi's portrait. A knock at the kitchen door.

HELEN: Yes, who is it?

SAMSON enters, carrying a box of balloons. He wears designer sunglasses.

Oh. Samson.

SAMSON: Good morning, Madam. Sorry I couldn't come sooner. About Papa…

HELEN: It's all right. Thank you.

SAMSON: I brought balloons for decorating the canopies. International quality.

HELEN: I will open Sola's room. Blow them up in there. *Oya,* there's no time.

SAMSON: Er, yes, Madam.

They exit upstairs. AFOLABI enters with suitcases. YINKA enters. He is dressed in a suit. He surveys the sitting-room with disgust. HELEN enters from upstairs, mobile phone in hand.

HELEN: What is the time that you're just coming… Oh, sorry, I thought it was the hairdresser. Welcome, Brother Yinka.

YINKA: Morning.

HELEN: When did you arrive? Oh of course you've just… (*To AFOLABI.*) Tell Ekong to collect the hairdresser. I've told her he's on his way.

AFOLABI exits.

How is your computer business? Papa was so proud when you opened a new branch –

YINKA: Fine.

HELEN: Yes, em, I had to get new material for the family uniforms.

YINKA: What of Soji?

HELEN: Brother Soji loves it. He says I have done Dad proud… Oh. He and Sola, they went out. They should be back soon.

The front door opens. SOJI enters.

(*Relieved.*) Ah-ha.

SOJI: Hey! The Black Republican has landed!

They hug.

YINKA: I want to talk to you – in private.

HELEN: (*Makes to leave reluctantly.*) What of Sola?

SOJI: She branched at her friend's. Wale…?

HELEN: (*As she exits upstairs.*) But I told her! What is wrong with this child? (*Phones.*)

SOJI: So Joyce couldn't make it after all.

YINKA: I know you can leave your sick mother to travel half-way round the world.

SOJI: You're only just telling me her mother's sick. You could have let the twins come. They wanted to.

YINKA: They're prepping for their exams. America doesn't reward failure.

SOJI: Living the dream, eh? Just like their father.

YINKA: (*Faces Chief Adeyemi's portrait.*) And their father's father. Soon the Adeyemi name will be as American as apple pie… So. The material.

SOJI: Yeah, um, it should be all right. Knowing Helen's taste in clothes.

YINKA: It's not the material we agreed on.

SOJI: She says they've all been worn before.

YINKA: She discussed it with you?

SOJI: After she... You know, the time factor. She had to make a decision.

YINKA: That's why we say you should get married. You keep discipline in a home. You control things. What other decisions has she made behind my back?

HELEN enters from upstairs.

HELEN: Brother Yinka. You didn't give me chance to explain about the material.

YINKA: There's no point now.

HELEN: There is, oh. I cannot go behind your back. No one can replace you as Papa's eldest son. (*Goes on her knees.*) Please, forgive me.

SOLA, PAKIMI and ABASINA, with the clothes, enter through front door. ABASINA exits to enter through kitchen. SOLA looks on in disgust.

PAKIMI: Brother Yinka, your stepmother accords you the respect your position deserves. Whatever she might have done, forgiveness is your only option.

YINKA: (*Stiffly.*) Okay.

HELEN stands up.

PAKIMI: God is in this house! Abasina bring the... Abasina!

ABASINA hands one outfit to PAKIMI. Puts the rest of the clothes on the sofa.

HELEN: Don't crease them, bush girl.

PAKIMI: You see how lovely they are? Fit for a king.

He hands the outfit to YINKA. YINKA turns his face. SOJI takes it from PAKIMI.

SOJI: Not bad.

YINKA eyes SOJI. SOJI hands the outfit to HELEN.

YINKA: I have to go freshen up. (*Exits upstairs.*)

ABASINA takes YINKA's bags upstairs.

PAKIMI: Well. I'd better keep an eye on the arrangements outside.

HELEN: Thank you, Pastor. (*Inspects the clothes.*)

PAKIMI exits.

SOLA: Back to being the housemaid, eh?

HELEN: Choose your words carefully my dear.

SOJI: Sometimes you have to sacrifice your pride –

SOLA: I am talking to my mother.

HELEN: Don't be rude to your elder brother! You are naïve. You cannot understand.

SOLA storms upstairs. SAMSON passes SOLA by.

SAMSON: Good morning, Sister.

SOLA ignores him. She exits.

SOJI: Excuse me. (*Goes after SOLA.*)

SAMSON: Good morning, Sir.

SOJI: Samson. (*Exits.*)

HELEN: Oh. (*Gives SAMSON a wad of notes from her handbag.*)

SAMSON: Thank you, Ma. I should be going –

HELEN: Ehen. Abasina!

ABASINA enters from kitchen. SAMSON is irritated.

I'm checking on the aunties. When the hairdresser arrives… (*Exits through kitchen.*)

ABASINA curtseys. SAMSON counts the money and pockets it. He brings out two mobile phones and checks them for messages.

ABASINA: Brother Samson. You dey avoid me?

SAMSON: I have a business appointment. I cannot stay to chat.

ABASINA: When you go give Mama her allowance?

SAMSON: Soon.

ABASINA: Which one be soon? Which money Mama dey take maintain herself?

SAMSON: (*Testily.*) I said soon! What is it? Ah! Because you live in big house you've become big madam?

ABASINA: So when I dey leave this big house?

SAMSON: You can't leave. The funeral.

ABASINA eyes him defiantly.

SAMSON: Okay if not for the Adeyemis, what of we your family? The bakery is not yet finished.

ABASINA: That one is for you and your family.

SAMSON: So your nephews are not your family any more? The boys should not go to school because you are too lazy to work?

ABASINA: Papa pay your school fees –

SAMSON: Don't tell me how to look after my children! If you don't want to contribute your share tell me.

ABASINA: I need money.

SAMSON: What for?

ABASINA: Na me work for my money.

SAMSON: You cannot spoil my progress because you want to wear new dress –

ABASINA: I talk say I wan' buy dress – ?

SAMSON: What of the new dress I gave you last month – ?

ABASINA: That rag wey your wife throw'ay?

SAMSON: My wife's name is Sister Anna. You can patch it up.

ABASINA: Why Sister Anna no patch am for me?

SAMSON: My wife is not your tailor.

ABASINA: Last year you say Madam will allow me to learn trade. Patience next door don learn tailoring. She don get shop. Next month she go marry.

SAMSON: This your salary, I'm saving it for you.

ABASINA: When value of naira dey fall every day?

SAMSON: Once I start my export business we will be cashing pounds and dollars.

ABASINA: So why you no do that business first?

SAMSON: You ask too many questions that don't concern you.

ABASINA: It concerns me. Even if naira na one thousand to one pound, inflation go useless di money. Na because everything too cost dat's why di workers dey strike. No save my money for me again. Tell Madam to pay me direct.

SAMSON: How can she pay you direct? I am the one who brought you here.

ABASINA: Na me dey work! Na my money.

SAMSON: It's because you are around these book people. You don't understand what they are saying. Your wings are getting too big. So I your elder brother, I cannot control you again? That is very bad, Abasina. That is very bad… Small. After the funeral I will find you another house. If you go now Madam will not patronise me again. You don't know how lucky you are. I'm coming from Ikoyi. Patrick rumpled Chief's *aso oke*.[1] Chief scraped his head with a broken bottle. (*Smirks.*) His head is like the map of Nigeria.

ABASINA: Just tell Mama to send medicine for Patrick.

SAMSON: This is the best time to be around. People will spray money. (*Phones.*)

1 Expensive woven cloth.

ABASINA: Who go spray house-girl?

SAMSON: You have eyes. Shake your bottom at the right man. If you were as smart as Madam Helen you could have become the next Mrs Adeyemi – (*On the phone.*) *Omo*-boy! Which one, now? Has the consignment landed?

SAMSON exits through kitchen. ABASINA looks after him in disgust. She looks at Chief's photograph. SOJI and SOLA enter from upstairs. ABASINA exits to kitchen.

SOLA: I should have stayed away.

SOJI: Just because of a few balloons?

SOLA: See how they messed up my room.

SOJI: What's really bugging you? Talk to me.

SOLA: You know why I liked your mother?

SOJI: You liked her? (*Sees that she is serious.*) You didn't know her.

SOLA: She had self-discipline. She knew what she wanted and wasn't afraid to say so. That's what everyone says about her.

SOJI: She was a hard woman.

SOLA: Hard. Not harsh. Papa was harsh.

SOJI: Semantically speaking. Helen's an easy ride…um, an easy-going mother. I'd have thought any child would love that in a parent.

SOLA: Isn't that why Papa replaced your mother with mine?

SOJI: You don't know what you're talking about.

SOLA: Oh yeah. I'm naïve.

SOJI: That's not what I meant.

SOLA: I've never felt I belonged. Papa… He just… It's like I was something that happened.

SOJI: Papa was like that to all of us. Where do you think Yinka got his attitude from? The funeral's getting to you. Come here. (*Drags her into his arms. Holds her tightly.*)

SOLA: You're the only one who makes me feel I belong. You're my one source of light. Erratic like NEPA...

SOJI: Oh, thanks.

SOLA: You'll step up for me when it matters. Because that's the kind of person you really are...

SOJI slackens his hold. SOLA tightens her hold. They kiss fiercely. A sound from upstairs. They release each other quickly. YINKA enters.

SOJI: Hey, bro'.

SOLA: (*Stiffly.*) Welcome Brother Yinka.

YINKA: It's now you decide to greet me.

SOLA: (*She heads for kitchen.*) I came down to get a drink.

YINKA: Ehn? (*Rages after her.*)

SOJI: Yinka, no! Yinka! (*Restrains YINKA.*)

YINKA: What an insult!

SOJI: Come on, man!

YINKA: I will show you your place! You and your mother!

SOLA: (*Runs to central table. Grabs the scissors.*) I am not like my mother.

YINKA: Oh, you think you're strong, eh? I will kill you!

SOLA: You can try.

SOJI: Yinka!

YINKA: I swear on my father's corpse, you will not spend one more night in this house! (*To SOJI.*) And what the hell are you doing with this interloper?

SOLA: You are a bastard.

YINKA lunges at SOLA. SOJI barely restrains him. PAKIMI enters. YINKA calms down.

PAKIMI: Is everything all right? I heard a commotion.

SOJI: Everything is fine.

PAKIMI: But Abasina said –

SOJI: How are the preparations going?

PAKIMI: We are almost done. The caterer has arrived, thank God… Sola, can I talk to you for one minute.

SOLA drops the scissors on the table. YINKA pushes SOJI.

SOJI: Hey! Easy.

YINKA: Your mother's usurper is swanning around like she owns the place and you're playing big brother to her bastard.

SOJI: Sola is our sis-…our half-sister.

YINKA: You know how these things go, especially when you're dealing with these parasites.

SOJI: This isn't the time –

YINKA: And when they steal everything Mother worked for?

SOJI: Helen can't go against Dad's will. What are you afraid of?

YINKA: She stole Dad from Mother. This time, no way! This is a fight to the death.

SOJI: We don't even know what's in the will.

YINKA: One kobo is too much for her. *We* are the true Adeyemis. Remember that.

SOJI: Living in New York's turned you into a drama queen.

YINKA: You want history to repeat itself? You'll see when that usurper and her…

HELEN enters from front door.

HELEN: My big brothers, you are here… Abasina!

ABASINA: (*As she enters from kitchen.*) Ma!

HELEN: Is this how to clean up?

ABASINA tidies up around them. She is in discomfort.

Brother Yinka, I was going to ask. How is Joyce's mother?

PAKIMI and SOLA enter from kitchen. SOLA goes straight upstairs. SOJI gazes after her.

YINKA: She's on dialysis.

They expect YINKA to continue...

SOJI: Erm, where's Ekong?

HELEN: I sent him to the hairdresser. They have both disappeared... Abasina. (*Points to the clothes.*)

ABASINA takes HELEN's outfit and follows HELEN upstairs. SOJI and YINKA make to leave.

PAKIMI: Just a few words. (*Beckons to them to sit down.*)

SOJI: I don't know what Sola told you but –

PAKIMI: This is another matter.

SOJI: Oh.

PAKIMI: I don't want to poke my nose in your family's affairs but I like to think I'm very close to you.

YINKA: You're our former driver.

PAKIMI: *Papa*'s former driver.

YINKA: Still.

PAKIMI: In your absence the shifting sands of time have not reduced the pressures of running the estate. There are those who are not satisfied with their God-given lot. Afolabi wants an astronomical rise in his salary.

SOJI: Afolabi was here before any of us. He knows this place inside out.

PAKIMI: Which is why we cannot afford for him to organise thieves to ransack the estate.

SOJI: Afolabi is not that kind of person.

PAKIMI: And King David did not plan for Uriah. I know how dear he is to you. But the estate needs young blood to maintain it effectively.

YINKA: You invited us to discuss Afolabi?

PAKIMI: As perceptive as ever. Just like your father… Er, you know how messy sharing property can get. I would like to help make a smooth transition.

SOJI: The days of miracles are long gone.

PAKIMI: I – My church, would like to buy some land of the estate. Just enough to build a new church. I'll pay the going rate.

YINKA: But you only just moved into a new building last year.

PAKIMI: My congregation has grown exponentially. We live in dire times. People need direction. They recognise me as God's true voice.

SOJI: This has nothing to do with the New Evangelicals? They've just bought the Owoloju's estate down the road.

PAKIMI: Visibility in a prime location such as this will accelerate my God-appointed mission. Selling some land will make you liquid. Money can be shared much more easily than property.

YINKA: This family has money. The land is not for sale.

SOJI: But we've enough land to make the Duke of Westminster look like a sharecropper. It's an offer to consider.

PAKIMI nods vigorously. YINKA eyes SOJI.

YINKA: (*Stands up.*) There is nothing to consider. God has blessed you. You have risen above your station, fair enough. But trying to get your hands on our father's land? You're stretching too far.

PAKIMI: I'm just saying that with you and Helen –

YINKA: Tell Helen my mother built this estate. She will not carve it up. I have my father's wake to attend. (*Heads upstairs.*) Soji.

PAKIMI: It has nothing to do with Helen…

SOJI: You only have to look at the garden to see what a worker Afolabi is. That vase, Afolabi bought it as a gift to Papa when I was born.

PAKIMI: You don't need to remind me, Brother Soji.

SOJI: Dad hated it but he kept it there as a sign of respect for the old man…

AFOLABI enters.

AFOLABI: (*Bows to SOJI. To PAKIMI.*) E', Sah, the canopy is doing jigi-jigi.

PAKIMI: (*Testily.*) There was nothing wrong with it before. *Oya.*

They exit. ABASINA enters from upstairs.

YINKA: (*From the landing.*) Soji!

SOJI: Bring our clothes up to my room. (*Goes upstairs.*)

HELEN and SOLA enter from downstairs. HELEN is half-dressed.

ABASINA: Yes, Sah. (*Gathers the clothes.*)

SOLA and SOJI smile at each other. HELEN clocks them. HELEN gestures to ask if the clothes are for SOJI and YINKA. ABASINA nods. HELEN dances. ABASINA exits upstairs.

HELEN: (*Dances as she sings.*) 'They took them, they took them,' … (*Notices that SOLA is looking upstairs.*) Hey, I don't like the closeness of you and your brother.

SOLA: You say you want us to be a family.

HELEN: And I also say you should be wary of them. They are the true sons of their mother.

SOLA: The true sons of their father.

HELEN: You too you are the true child of your father, even more than them… *Oya, oya,* change. You cannot be late for your father's wake. (*Finishes dressing up.*)

SOLA: If you hadn't turned my room into a store –

ABASINA enters from upstairs.

HELEN: You didn't see my own room? It's a small sacrifice to make for your father. Hurry up!

SOLA: Abasina. (*Exits upstairs.*)

ABASINA stumbles with weariness as she takes the clothes.

HELEN: Suit yourself… What is wrong with you? *Abi*, those garage boys have been putting their penises inside you that you cannot walk properly again? Prostitute. Let me smell pregnancy on you, you will be out on the street where you belong. Get out of my sight!

ABASINA exits. HELEN puts on make-up. PAKIMI enters. HELEN gestures to him that Soji's and Yinka's clothes are gone.

PAKIMI: They took them? Hallelujah! The Lord has ordained it that today shall go without problem.

HELEN: Amen!

PAKIMI: (*Looks at HELEN appreciatively.*) The trouble with beauty is that it is beautiful.

HELEN: When last did I hear that?

PAKIMI: Papa said it enough times. How he kept so honest… I'm sorry. I didn't mean it that way.

HELEN: Lomi, we are not children. Someone put kola-nut in my mouth, I should not chew? Those boys cannot understand. Their father came to me.

PAKIMI: Every child thinks their mother is Virgin Mary.

HELEN: Mama Yinka[2] was no Virgin Mary. Not to us.

PAKIMI: She was not an easy woman.

HELEN: You've not forgotten.

PAKIMI: Still, we are examples that anybody can rise above their station, no matter what any man thinks.

HELEN: You mean no matter what Yinka thinks. I washed the wet dreams from his pants. And he wants me to continue worshipping him like that house-girl of before.

PAKIMI: (*Looks up warily to the stairs.*) Before you came in, I was talking with him.

2 Yinka's mother

HELEN: I am ready for them. My daughter will claim her rights to the estate.

PAKIMI: The idea is not to divide the estate like gamblers casting lots.

HELEN: My husband will not leave me empty-handed.

PAKIMI: We need to be sure.

HELEN: I am not like Mama Yinka. I'm not a prim sexless killjoy. She turned the whole house to monastery. You saw how much Papa and I enjoyed life together. It was then that people knew how rich he was. I set him free.

PAKIMI: Still, his mind was on other things. He told me –

HELEN: Lomi, I will bury my husband like a king. That is how we lived. They will read the will. I will claim my share. His sons have no choice –

PAKIMI: Listen to me, for once! God! See now, you've made me take the Lord's name in vain…

SOLA and ABASINA enter from upstairs. SOLA is dressed in her aso ebi.

Ah, my daughter. Any man who sees you will proclaim he has seen an angel.

HELEN: Pastor is complimenting you. You can at least smile.

SOLA: I thought this was a wake.

The sound of the funeral trumpet. Singing. YINKA and SOJI, on the landing. They are wearing identical attires, made from the old material. SOJI fiddles with his iPod as they descend.

HELEN: Brother Yinka, I thought we had resolved the matter.

PAKIMI: Brother Yinka. It is not right for the family to wear different uniforms. People will pick up the wrong signal.

HELEN: Brother Soji. Help us beg Brother Yinka. Not today. Your father will not look kindly on us –

YINKA takes Chief Adeyemi's portrait. Nods to SOJI to take their family portrait.

I begged you. On my knees…

YINKA and SOJI exit through front door. SOLA lets out a cynical laugh and exits.

PAKIMI: Don't worry. We will sort this out. (*Sings, gestures to HELEN join in.*)

PAKIMI leads HELEN out. She returns to take her family portrait and exits.

The music fades.

THE FUNERAL

The following day, afternoon. ABASINA and AFOLABI enter from kitchen with party utensils. They adorn the walls with a funeral poster of Chief Adeyemi and balloons. ABASINA is still feeling queasy.

AFOLABI: Don't worry. When the party start and the big men spray you with money, your stomach will settle.

ABASINA: Baba!

AFOLABI: Big man doesn't care if you are from village or you are ground-nut seller. If he like your face…

ABASINA: Baba! Heyi-ay!

AFOLABI: Abasina. You are good girl but don't pretend that you are little child. As Madam was house-girl yesterday, see her today. Fine girl like you, you just have to know the right man. Have patience…

ABASINA casts a quick glance at the poster of Chief Adeyemi. EKONG enters.

EKONG: Your own kind of patience, even Job did not have.

ABASINA: Mr Ekong! Dem don finish for church?

EKONG: Madam say make I help you. She go phone when service end. (*Puts on music.*) Party don start! (*Dances. Takes a bottle of beer. Raises a toast to Chief Adeyemi's poster.*) To the Big Man… Abasina, dance with me.

AFOLABI: What is wrong with this man?

ABASINA: Mr Ekong!

EKONG: (*Swirls ABASINA around.*) For now, we are the owners of Adeyemi Estate. Afolabi, come on. *Ariya!*

AFOLABI: I know my place.

EKONG: Stay there, then. (*Continues dancing with ABASINA.*)

ABASINA: Oh! Mr Ekong, I no well.

EKONG: Your illness is too much work. Enjoyment is the cure. (*Releases her. Dances on his own.*)

AFOLABI: Some people don't know their place.

EKONG: What-ti! You that you know your place, what is your gain?

AFOLABI: Wait and see.

EKONG: See this old man. You think say Papa put you for him will?

AFOLABI: You can laugh. But you will see who will laugh longest.

EKONG: A fool at forty is a fool –

ABASINA: Mr Ekong!

AFOLABI: Your father is a fool!

EKONG: Yes! He is a fool! 'Yes Sah, no Ma' all his life. And what is his reward? House-boy at age of seventy! Abasina, don't listen to this Yoruba man. That is how they do for their country.

AFOLABI: And your father who is doing 'yes Sah, no Ma' is Yoruba?

ABASINA: (*Turns off the music. Firmly.*) Stop this nonsense! Mr Ekong, we don finish for here. Make you return to the church.

EKONG: (*Mock salute.*) Yes 'Madam'. (*Exits with the beer.*)

AFOLABI: You young people. You don't listen to your elders. Have patience. Or all your hard work, another person will reap your reward.

ABASINA: Baba. I've heard you. I am not a small girl.

AFOLABI: You are taking your countryman side. Is okay. (*In anger exits through front door.*)

ABASINA: Baba...

Funeral trumpet. AFOLABI runs back in and exits through kitchen. The noise of people outside partying. Enter HELEN, SOLA, YINKA, SOJI and PAKIMI. ABASINA takes the portraits and hangs them back on the wall.

HELEN: Thank God. Power Holdings has not taken the light.

PAKIMI: They know what day today is.

HELEN: I've just buried my husband.

YINKA glares at HELEN. EKONG enters.

EKONG: E', Sah, Lawyer Anike have arrive.

YINKA: Er, all right. (*As he passes EKONG, hisses.*) Broadcast it to whole world!

EKONG scratches his head apologetically. YINKA and EKONG exit. HELEN looks at PAKIMI. She is agitated.

PAKIMI: He can't do anything about the will. Come on. Papa is looking down upon us from Heaven. He will not like this nonsense... Okay, I'll keep an eye on him –

AFOLABI peers through the front door.

Yes?

AFOLABI: Retired General Olowonjaiye, Sah...

PAKIMI: Ah! (*Exits through front door. Off.*) My General! Welcome. Helen!

HELEN eyes SOJI. She touches Chief Adeyemi's portrait as she exits through front door. SOLA flops onto the sofa.

SOLA: Your brother...

SOJI: Yinka is just being Yinka.

SOLA: You won't go and look after your guests?

SOJI: Are you chasing me away?

SOLA: We should be out there. We'll have all the time in the world after today. I'll be so glad. The first place I want to see is your office. Then I want to ride on the Millennium Wheel. Then I'll invite all my friends to our place...

SOJI: Are you crazy?

SOLA: They don't know. (*Laughs.*) You should see the look on your face.

SOJI: It might be a good idea to finish your studies. There's no point running away to start all over again.

SOLA: That's not what we agreed on.

SOJI: Yeah but one more semester won't kill you…

HELEN enters.

HELEN: People are asking of you. Sola, your 'friend' Wale is here.

SOLA gets up.

(*Jokingly.*) I don't want grandchildren yet, oh!

SOLA ignores her and exits.

Erm, Brother Soji. Brother Yinka is paying too much attention to the lawyer. He should show respect for your father. The will we can sort out after the party. People are talking.

SOJI: Not even Yinka can get Lawyer Anike to change the will. Don't worry.

ABASINA enters from kitchen.

HELEN: All our guests have been served?

ABASINA: Yes, Ma. E', Sah, your uncles want to see you.

ABASINA exits through kitchen.

SOJI: (*Stands up.*) He's like a soldier. Papa always joked that Yinka should have been named Soji.

HELEN: But he is going beyond a joke. People will say Papa has died, the family is falling apart.

SOJI: That's their problem. (*Heads for front door.*)

HELEN: Remember: Sola is also your flesh and blood.

SOJI pauses briefly. PAKIMI enters. They greet each other. PAKIMI waits. SOJI exits.

PAKIMI: He's still with the lawyer…

EKONG enters through kitchen with a tray. He takes some drinks and exits.

HELEN: You are right. I will not allow him to ruin this day for me. Let him scheme all he wants. Chief Adeyemi will do me right. We have prayed over it.

PAKIMI: It is in times of uncertainty that our faith is tested. I too believe that Papa will treat you fairly. But what fair means to Papa we don't know.

HELEN: Now you are making me worried again.

PAKIMI: You know better than anyone how volatile Papa could be.

HELEN: I know he would not make his wife a laughing stock.

PAKIMI: That is our prayer… I have a proposal. Something that will secure your future and Sola's in the event of the unexpected…

HELEN: Yes? *Oya,* Pastor, I have to see to my guests –

PAKIMI: Marry me.

HELEN: Sorry?

PAKIMI: It makes sense. This is –

HELEN: I am burying my husband!

PAKIMI: Stop playing games! This is what we've always wanted.

HELEN: (*Points outside.*) And you've forgotten about Mrs Pakimi. And your children.

PAKIMI: They will understand.

HELEN: Oh, and what about your church?

PAKIMI: I am the church, the church is me. My members will kick a fuss but dust settles.

HELEN: You see me fighting one battle you want me to fight another?

ABASINA enters. Takes one of the coolers and exits.

(*Defiant.*) If Yinka is talking to the lawyer, I will join him! (*Exits.*)

PAKIMI: Helen! Helen!

PAKIMI exits. YINKA enters from kitchen, with a whisky bottle. He makes sure no one is around. He exits upstairs, taking a swig along the way. Enter ABASINA, with a tray. She puts drinks on it and waits to see if anyone is coming in. She exits upstairs. HELEN and PAKIMI enter, followed by EKONG.

HELEN: You are sure Brother Yinka came in here?

EKONG: Yes, Madam. Maybe he is upstairs –

HELEN: Who asked you? (*Clocks the tray.*) Why did you leave the tray there?

EKONG: Not me, Madam –

HELEN: Take it out, idiot!

EKONG takes the tray and exits. HELEN marches upstairs.

PAKIMI: Mama Sola…

The lights go out. A cry of 'NEPA!' fills the air. A generator roars into life. The lights come back on. The lights flicker violently and go out. An explosion. Commotion.

HELEN: Jesus! What was that?

EKONG enters from kitchen with a torch, candles and matches.

EKONG: E', Sah, the generator has blow.

PAKIMI: (*Takes the torch from EKONG.*) Stay here.

HELEN and PAKIMI exit. EKONG makes sure they are gone and takes some food. He puts something in his mouth, spits it out. He looks for the candle. ABASINA creeps downstairs. He lights it just as ABASINA collides with him.

EKONG: Yah! Abasina! You want to kill me?

ABASINA: Sorry, Mr Ekong.

EKONG: Ah-ah… Where you hide yourself?

ABASINA: Sister Sola send me errand.

EKONG: Is not the drinks she ask you to collect? Abasina, answer me…

YINKA enters from upstairs. He smoothes his clothes.

YINKA: What was that?

EKONG: The generator, Sah.

YINKA: For goodness' sake. (*Exits.*)

ABASINA makes to leave. EKONG holds her back.

EKONG: Abasina. *Abasina.* Don't say I don't tell you. The game you are playing with these people. Okay-oh. When the grass fight the elephant suffers, *abi* how dem dey talk am?

ABASINA: Madam will be looking for me. (*Exits.*)

Sound of the family seeing off guests by the front door. EKONG quickly wipes his mouth. HELEN, SOJI, SOLA, PAKIMI enter with AFOLABI. HELEN leads AFOLABI to sit on the sofa.

HELEN: They're all going to the other parties now…

AFOLABI: (*Makes himself comfortable.*) Thank you, Madam.

HELEN: Abasina! Ekong, go and call Abasina.

EKONG: Yes, Madam. (*Exits through kitchen.*)

SOJI: (*To AFOLABI.*) If you hadn't ripped out the plug –

HELEN: Don't blame me! Alhaji has never sold adulterated diesel. Everybody knows that.

SOJI: And I suppose this is a new kind of diesel?

HELEN: You, big Professor, ask your useless president why there is petrol shortage. I only wanted to give your father a proper burial.

SOJI: He really went out with a bang!

SOLA: I didn't see you planning the funeral…

ABASINA and EKONG enter.

PAKIMI: If we can just calm down –

HELEN: (*To ABASINA.*) Where did you go? I will deal with you later. Get food for Mr Afolabi.

ABASINA gets food from the cooler.

(*To EKONG.*) Ehen? You didn't see what happened? Go and help!

EKONG exits. AFOLABI smirks.

PAKIMI: Afolabi. Join him.

SOJI: Let the old man eat now.

PAKIMI: He should be helping Ekong to clear up. (*Claps his hands at AFOLABI.*)

AFOLABI exits through kitchen.

HELEN: Pastor…

PAKIMI: A befitting ending to his triumphant entry.

SOLA takes the food from ABASINA and exits through kitchen.

SOJI: You didn't need to do that. He saved us.

PAKIMI: God saved us.

SOJI: What is it with you and Afolabi –

PAKIMI: I think we should exert our energies more productively other than talking about the help.

HELEN: Thank God nobody is injured. What a day.

SOJI heads for the front door.

Brother Soji…

SOJI: I have to see off my uncles. (*Exits.*)

HELEN: People will say look at the send-off I gave to Papa.

PAKIMI: Those same people who said Papa lowered his standards when he married you? Forget them, my dear.

HELEN: This way I could have showed them who I am.

PAKIMI: You cannot change people's minds.

HELEN: I would have proved that Papa made the right choice.

PAKIMI: You make a choice, you live with it.

HELEN: (*Jumps up.*) Hepa! They are talking to the lawyer. (*Makes to storm out.*)

YINKA and SOJI enter.

Why don't you stop playing games? We are all adults.

YINKA: If saying goodbye to our uncles is a game to you/

HELEN: I am not a fool. Let us call Lawyer Anike and the accountant. We will settle everything tomorrow.

YINKA: Why wait? They are still here. Soji…

SOJI reluctantly exits.

There is blood and there is blood. Tonight we will find out which is which.

Later that night. All the family except for YINKA. The atmosphere is glum. Some lanterns and candles provide light. Suddenly the lights come back on. A cheer of 'NEPA!' in the distance. Documents dangle from HELEN's limp hand. ABASINA takes out the lanterns and returns to clean up. AFOLABI takes some coolers and exits through kitchen.

HELEN: Today should have ended in darkness. It would have been appropriate.

SOJI: Don't let Rafiu hear you say that. You should have seen him when Ekong announced the party is over. Ekong is not wise, oh. You don't tell a hungry man who's just loaded his plate, '*oya*, start going home'. Especially when his teeth are as sharp as Rafiu's.

HELEN: This is not the time for jokes.

SOJI: But you're all smiling now. See, see, see…

They burst out laughing. YINKA walks in, torch in one hand, a whisky bottle in the other. He shows signs of drunkenness. ABASINA takes the torch from him. She puts it in the kitchen and returns to clean.

YINKA: You've done your job. You can now laugh over my parents' graves.

HELEN: Me? What have I done –

YINKA: Looter!

SOLA: Don't insult my mother!

YINKA: Shut your mouth!

SOJI: Yinka calm down –

YINKA: You heard the accountant! She bankrupted Papa.

HELEN: I didn't have access to his accounts. I asked for money, he gave me.

YINKA: You asked for everything! My dear, all the gold in Ghana cannot cover up your background.

HELEN: Your jealousy has turned your head.

YINKA: (*Approaches.*) Who are you calling mad?

HELEN: (*Stands up. Ties her headgear round her waist.*) Who is a looter?

SOJI: (*Restrains YINKA.*) For God's sake, both of you! Sola take your mother upstairs. Go on!

HELEN: I'm not leaving this room for anybody! This is my house!

YINKA: This is my father's house.

SOLA leads her mother upstairs.

HELEN: This is my house! Nobody can take it from me!

SOJI: (*To ABASINA, who continues cleaning.*) Madam, you want your own invite? Get…!

ABASINA exits.

Man what's your problem?

YINKA: I told you this would happen.

SOJI: It's not as bad as it looks.

YINKA: Were you deaf? Didn't you hear the accountant?

SOJI: After Thanksgiving we'll talk to him. There has to be something left. He was drunk.

YINKA: If you had to inform your biggest client that they are now paupers, would you do it sober? We are not selling the estate. No way.

SOJI: That was only a suggestion. Like selling the office blocks off to those South African investors.

YINKA: I thought dealing with Afrikaners was anathema to you.

SOJI: We're all Africans now. Or those Chinese businessmen. The factories are just what they're looking for.

YINKA: They're shells. They've been dormant for the past five years.

SOJI: You're joking!

YINKA: You never concerned yourself… I don't understand. Every time I asked Dad how is business, he'd say things were looking up.

SOJI: But he was spending money like he owned the mint.

YINKA: Bank loans.

SOJI: But if he wasn't credit-worthy how was he –

YINKA: Soji, we're in Nigeria.

SOJI: God…

HELEN: (*Off.*) I say I don't need to lie down!

YINKA: I need some air. (*Runs through the front door.*)

HELEN and SOLA come down the stairs.

HELEN: After all I've done for you boys. Treated you like my own sons. Abasina!

ABASINA: (*From the kitchen.*) Ma! (*Enters.*) Ma?

HELEN: Is this how to clean up?

ABASINA resumes cleaning. There is a loud crash in the direction of the front door.

Yeh! What is that again?

HELEN and ABASINA exit. SOLA heads for the front door. SOJI grabs her arm.

SOJI: You all right?

SOLA: Yes.

SOJI: How will you cope?

SOLA: (*Squeezes his hand.*) You mean how will we cope?

HELEN and PAKIMI enter holding YINKA who clutches his head. ABASINA gets a first-aid box. HELEN tends to YINKA.

HELEN: Why didn't you come out? (*To ABASINA.*) Tell Ekong to get the car ready.

ABASINA exits.

YINKA: (*Stiffly.*) I said I'm fine.

SOJI: What happened?

PAKIMI: The work of your friend Afolabi. Brother Yinka leaned against the canopy.

HELEN: If you're sure…

SOLA: (*Angrily.*) Brother Yinka says he's fine! (*Exits upstairs.*)

HELEN: I'm only asking. If you need me. (*Exits upstairs.*)

SOJI: Thanks, Mama Sola.

PAKIMI: Mama Sola was only looking after you, as she has done in the past… Perhaps I too can play a similar role in a more perilous situation.

SOJI: How did you –

YINKA: Don't be stupid. Helen has gone blabbering to him. Forget it.

PAKIMI: Once the banks turn on you, you will find them hard bargainers.

YINKA: The banks can't touch this property.

PAKIMI: This estate is the jewel in the crown. The debts are in the family name. You are liable.

YINKA: We will pay what we owe the banks. Papa's London house is worth a few pounds.

PAKIMI: Papa sold it to service his foreign debts.

YINKA looks at SOJI.

SOJI: Dad gave the keys to his estate agent! I had no reason to go there –

PAKIMI: My offer still stands. I need only a few plots.

YINKA: Let's say I agree to sell the whole estate?

SOJI: Woh, woh, woh! The whole estate?

PAKIMI: (*Eyes light up.*) I would table a suitable offer… There will be lots of paperwork.

YINKA: I'm not in a hurry to return to New York.

PAKIMI: What about Helen?

YINKA: I'm head of this family.

Pause. They shake hands.

PAKIMI: I will have a word with her. If you don't mind.

YINKA shrugs, starts drinking whisky.

Brother Soji. (*Exits upstairs.*)

SOJI: You need a brain scan.

YINKA: With all our debts, the estate is a burden. Not another kobo is going on maintaining her. She has stolen enough already. We pay her off, she finds her way.

SOJI: What about Joyce and the boys? Who's looking after your business?

YINKA: I'll sort that out. It's time I had a branch in Nigeria, anyway.

SOJI: What about me?

YINKA: When I built my house, what were you doing? Too busy playing *Baba* London.

SOJI: And now that we have to sell Dad's other properties do I build my house in the sky?

YINKA: You can stay in my guest-house when you visit –

SOJI: I was hoping… You know that government programme? The one where they bring home professionals from abroad?

YINKA: You applied for it?

SOJI nods.

Your reason being?

SOJI: I just want to come home.

YINKA: It's a good gig. You get paid in dollars, right? I thought you were happy in London with your new job.

SOJI: Yeah, well. Don't tell anyone yet. It's not been finalised.

YINKA: Anyway, you'll help me sort out this mess. One thing is certain: you won't be living here. I've got to call Joyce.

Exits upstairs with the whisky. He passes PAKIMI and HELEN, who are on their way down.

PAKIMI: Brother Soji, I hope all is well.

SOJI: I'm fine. The air-conditioning needs fixing.

HELEN: We're giving it a rest. What with the light coming and going.

SOJI: It's as if Mother's back in charge.

PAKIMI: Times have changed…

SOJI eyes PAKIMI.

SOJI: The driver is in the driving seat. (*Exits through front door.*) If anybody wants me, I've gone for a walk.

HELEN looks at PAKIMI questioningly.

PAKIMI: (*Dismissive.*) He's talking professor-talk. I didn't want Sola to hear us, that's why I wanted us to come downstairs.

HELEN: I still don't feel comfortable about letting Afolabi go.

PAKIMI: He has served his time.

HELEN: I have a father. How is he going to feed?

PAKIMI: He has children. Let them perform their God-given duty and take care of him.

HELEN: The country is tough. Sons are kicking out their mothers –

PAKIMI: And that is your number one problem?

HELEN: Honestly I didn't know about Papa's finances. He never breathed a word to me. Where did it all go? Honest money should be solid as a rock.

PAKIMI: Papa was a businessman.

HELEN: Are you saying he was not honest? His body is not yet cold you dare speak ill of him! You a pastor. Were you not the one who drove him to his business meetings with foreign businessmen?

PAKIMI: So? Oh, because they are white they are honest? Businessmen speak only one language. (*Gestures money.*)

HELEN: (*Heads for the stairs.*) If this is the nonsense you brought me down to hear –

PAKIMI: Yinka is selling the estate.

HELEN: (*Stops and turns round.*) Now you are trying to be funny.

PAKIMI: I will help you negotiate a decent pay-off.

HELEN: I am not a harlot that they can pay off! I am Chief Olanrewaju Adeyemi's lawfully wedded wife!

YINKA appears on the landing.

YINKA: Stop shouting in my father's house.

HELEN: You cannot make me homeless, you hear?

YINKA: I am the man of this house.

HELEN: Man? Who made you into a man?

YINKA: Spread your poisonous lies.

HELEN takes off her wrapper.

PAKIMI: Helen! (*Holds her arm.*)

HELEN: (*Breaks free. Shouts.*) Everybody come and see the woman who made Yinka Adeyemi into a man! (*Removes her buba.*)

PAKIMI locks the front door. EKONG puts his head through kitchen door. PAKIMI waves EKONG back into the kitchen. SOLA appears at the top of the stairs. YINKA trembles.

Adeyinka Adeyemi, come down and see! (*Removes her petticoat.*) Small boy!

YINKA: Bitch.

HELEN: Your mother is a bitch.

PAKIMI: Helen it is enough!

YINKA descends. PAKIMI comes between them.

HELEN: What? What do you want to do? Everything my father this, my father that! My father my father my father! Go back to Yankee and sort your life out, small boy! You should have seen him on our first night. (*Gestures holding a penis.*) 'Where do I put it?' Me and you. God punish you…

YINKA: You are leaving this house today.

YINKA marches back upstairs. SOLA smirks at him. YINKA glares at her as he walks past. SOLA descends. She kisses her mother and exits.

PAKIMI: What was that for?

HELEN: (*Puts her clothes back on.*) You are trying to understand Sola? You didn't see me in my best light.

PAKIMI: I beg to disagree… But you and him?

HELEN: Don't pretend you don't know.

PAKIMI: Actually I didn't –

HELEN: What do I do now?

PAKIMI: You won't be homeless. You've got your own lovely house.

HELEN: I'm too young to return to my village. Help me find out who they sold the estate to. Maybe I can do a deal with them.

PAKIMI: I think that offer has expired.

HELEN: Just help me find out. You don't know how much this pains me.

PAKIMI: I have to prepare for the Thanksgiving.

HELEN: You were going to tell me something.

PAKIMI: Tomorrow.

HELEN: What of our prayers?

PAKIMI: Tomorrow, tomorrow... (*Exits.*)

An hour later.

ABASINA and AFOLABI enter from kitchen with coolers and other items from the party. She makes sure no one is around, puts rice in a container and gives it to AFOLABI.

AFOLABI: Behaving as if he is the owner of the estate. Just because Chief's sons are not around. And I am the one who save them, oh. I risk my life.

ABASINA: God will reward you, Baba.

AFOLABI: Is not God reward I'm looking for now.

ABASINA: Why Pastor no like you?

AFOLABI: I don't know what I did for him.

ABASINA: Maybe you know his secret...

AFOLABI: I am not gossip like woman. (*Eats.*)

ABASINA: Okay then, gossip like man. He dey tief?

AFOLABI shakes his head.

He dey tell lie?

AFOLABI shakes his head.

He sleep with Mama Yinka?

AFOLABI eyes her.

So wetin he do now! Eh, Baba, you know say, breakfast for this house no dey easy to find. (*Pulls a serious face.*)

AFOLABI: (*Smiles.*) He and Mama Sola –

ABASINA: Old news. I even believe say dem dey bang each other before Papa die.

AFOLABI: Don't talk nonsense.

ABASINA: How many special prayer does one person need?

AFOLABI: When you are talking nonsense talk why Madam will not treat you bad?

ABASINA: You talk nonsense talk about Pastor?

AFOLABI: That is different. Now that Papa's children are here, Pastor have no role in this house again. That's why I don't say anything to him. My time has come.

ABASINA: Ah, Baba, you never hear about the will –

EKONG enters. His hand is bandaged.

EKONG: The triumphant entry. That is your nickname from now forever.

AFOLABI: That is your grandfather's nickname!

ABASINA: Wetin! (*Points to upstairs.*) *Oya*, everybody outside.

EKONG: (*Serves himself rice in a container.*) Any news?

ABASINA: About what?

EKONG: The will now. Is it not the reason why Madam and Brother dey fight?

AFOLABI: Fight? When?

ABASINA: Dem dey sell the estate to Pastor.

EKONG: Talk true!

AFOLABI: That is lie.

ABASINA: I hear Pastor and Brother Yinka as dem make agreement. Baba, Pastor no dey go anywhere.

AFOLABI: I say that is lie!

YINKA: (*On the landing.*) Who is there?

ABASINA and EKONG scramble into the kitchen. YINKA with the whisky bottle descends. He is drunk. AFOLABI realises the truth.

AFOLABI: Is me, Sir. I'm looking for Brother Soji.

YINKA: You see him here?

SOJI enters.

Ah, Afolabi. You are a conjurer. (*Prostrates to AFOLABI.*) All hail, Afolabi, the Professor Peller[3] of Adeyemi Estate!

SOJI: Come back later.

AFOLABI exits. SOJI pulls YINKA up onto the sofa.

YINKA: Yo! What's up, man?

SOJI: Pull yourself together.

YINKA: (*Laugh.*) Hey, look at that, Soji giving orders. The world has truly turned upside down.

SOJI: You need to sober up.

YINKA: You are right not to marry! Women, they are a curse. Black women, don't go near them. They will poison you. When they do this (*Waves his finger and rolls his head.*) run! Run!

SOJI: (*Tries to take him upstairs.*) Come on.

YINKA: (*Pushes SOJI away.*) I must warn all men. Run, guys or they will kill you! (*Collapses into the sofa.*) I'm the true son of my father! There I am building the American wing of the Adeyemi dynasty. Oh yes, in God's Own Country. In God's Own Goddamn Country. My friend! To have family in another man's land is not good. I love my boys. But they pledge allegiance to the Stars and Stripes. Soon they'll go off

3 Famous Nigerian magician

to fight in Iraq. But their women, ho, ho! Marrying African American is the same as marrying African. (*Makes the sound of a buzzer.*) Wrong! Don't believe them when they tell you we're all from the source. They are American, end of story. It's amazing. So, because a man has a ring on his finger he cannot look at another woman, eh?

SOJI: Yinka, you're not making sense.

YINKA: A man cannot have a meaningless fling, just to keep his manhood ticking? Except that his own wife must pull him down… Did we qualify for the World Cup…?

SOJI: (*Shakes YINKA.*) Yinka. Yinka! What's going on with you and Joyce?

YINKA: Who? Oh, *Joyce*! She's filed for divorce. She is taking everything. The house, the kids, the business. That same Joyce. Behaving as if she is the first African God put on this earth. She meant nothing to me I pleaded with this woman. Twenty years of marriage, burst like a bubble. It's my fault. Papa warned me: don't get involved with foreigners. They don't understand our way. I said, 'Papa, Joyce is one of us.' He said, 'You are stupid for thinking so.' Papa. Papa, Papa, Papa… Always listen to your father. Black man, you are on your own!

SOJI: Get up.

YINKA: I'm okay here.

SOJI: The others will see you.

YINKA: Let them. They've stripped me naked already.

SOJI: Come on…

YINKA shoves SOJI away. YINKA puts his head in his hands and sobs. ABASINA enters from kitchen.

ABASINA: Is not good for people to see you like this, Sah. (*She holds out her hand.*)

YINKA takes her hand. SOLA enters through front door. ABASINA leads YINKA upstairs. On the landing:

67

YINKA: I've told you. When we're alone, don't call me 'Sir'.

SOJI: Not a word.

SOLA: (*Smirking.*) Did I say anything?

SOJI looks at her. SOLA bursts out laughing.

SOJI: You think it's funny?

SOLA: You should have been here a few minutes ago. Your brother, he wants his women subservient. Just like Papa.

SOJI: And what do you want?

SOLA: I've got him right here. (*Hugs him.*)

SOJI: And what about Wale?

SOLA: Just a friend.

SOJI: Just a friend you spent nearly all of the party with.

SOLA: He's my standby generator. In case you do a Soji on me.

SOJI: A Soji…

AFOLABI enters. They break away quickly. AFOLABI turns his face.

AFOLABI: I will come back, Sah.

SOJI: No, no, it's all right. How can I help you?

SOLA goes upstairs. There is a smile on her face.

AFOLABI: I hope I'm not disturbing you.

SOJI: No, no. Please sit down.

AFOLABI: I don't want to dirty the chair.

SOJI: All right then. Something to drink?

AFOLABI: Thank you, Sah. I can take stout back to boys quarters. Big stout.

SOJI: What can I do for you?

AFOLABI: Pastor want to sack me.

SOJI: Oh. You've heard. He's not sacking you. He's laying you off.

AFOLABI: What is the difference? I am the one who make the garden and the lawn. The tree that you and Brother Yinka are using to make swing. I am the one who plant it.

SOJI: I know.

AFOLABI: (*Picks up the vase.*) And this vase. I am the one who buy it for Papa the day you are born.

SOJI: Yes, yes.

AFOLABI: I don't know what I did to Pastor. Person who work supposed to reap his reward. I work very hard for your father. And of all his children you are the one I am close to. That's why I come to you, nobody else.

SOJI: I know that.

AFOLABI: You remember you say you are going to save the whole Nigeria? You remember? I am not even asking for that one. Just help me talk to Pastor. Is only this work that is keeping me alive.

SOJI: I'm sorry I can't help you.

AFOLABI: Please now! (*Weeps. prostrates at SOJI's feet.*)

SOJI: Mr Afolabi!

AFOLABI: Please, I'm begging you!

SOJI: Mr Afolabi, please stand up. Please.

AFOLABI: Where can I go after this? Where can I go?

SOJI: (*Pulls him up.*) I'll talk to Pastor. Just get up.

AFOLABI: (*Stands up. Still weeping.*) Thank you, Sah.

SOJI: It's okay.

AFOLABI: As you have spoken, God has already reward your good heart. (*Polishes the vase with his sleeve as he heads for the kitchen.*)

SOJI: Uh-huh, uh-huh.

AFOLABI: Thank you. (*Exits. Returns to take the Guinness and exits through kitchen.*)

SOJI goes upstairs. ABASINA comes down. SOJI looks at her. ABASINA averts her gaze.

SOJI: Make sure you turn off all the lights.

ABASINA curtseys. SOJI goes upstairs, turns round and looks at ABASINA. ABASINA turns off the lights, leaving SOJI in darkness.

THANKSGIVING

The next morning. ABASINA is tidying up. Enter HELEN. She is dressed to go out.

HELEN: You are sure Pastor has not called this morning?

ABASINA: Yes, Madam.

HELEN takes the car keys. ABASINA exits to kitchen.

HELEN: Where are you going?

ABASINA: To call Ekong, Madam.

HELEN: Did I ask you to call him? Moron. (*Exits.*)

ABASINA continues cleaning. EKONG rushes in, chewing-stick in mouth.

EKONG: I hear motor.

ABASINA: Is Madam.

EKONG races out.

ABASINA: She no ask for you!

EKONG returns, looks at his bandaged hand.

EKONG: Dat Rafiu na animal. If you see am yesterday. (*Growls like a dog.*)

ABASINA: No wake up the house! Madam has her own problem.

EKONG: She must have big problem to leave so early when we have Thanksgiving. Maybe is to look for where she and Sola go live.

ABASINA: I know?

EKONG searches the table.

Mr Ekong, you keep something there?

EKONG: Abasina, you have sorted yourself.

AFOLABI enters. EKONG picks up the vase.

AFOLABI: Has Brother Soji come down?

ABASINA: Not yet. Sorry Baba… Mr Ekong!

EKONG: This one is my compensation. Afolabi, you no go take something for yourself?

AFOLABI: (*Blocks his path.*) Put it back!

EKONG: Brother Soji cannot help you, my friend.

AFOLABI: Put it back!

EKONG: Old man, you want to fight me?

AFOLABI: I'm telling you now!

EKONG: (*Puts back the vase.*) Is not me that will kill you. Is your blindness that will kill you. (*Exits.*)

SOJI and SOLA on the landing. SOJI sees AFOLABI and retreats, pulling SOLA back.

AFOLABI: I will come back later. (*Exits.*)

SOLA and SOJI come downstairs.

ABASINA: Good morning, Sah, good morning, Sista.

SOLA: Morning. Get our breakfast.

ABASINA enters kitchen.

This could be our last breakfast together in this house.

SOJI: You still haven't told me what you plan to do.

SOLA: What we plan to do. I'm sensing another power outage.

SOJI: London's not all rosy. My life's not going the way I thought it would.

SOLA: Look at how messed up this country is. Everybody wants to check out. Didn't your friends tell you?

SOJI: Yeah but home is home isn't it? For better for worse.

SOLA: Nothing can be worse than not knowing where your next meal is coming from.

ABASINA enters with the breakfast. She exits to kitchen.

I hope she hasn't puked in it.

SOJI looks quizzically.

You wouldn't know morning sickness if it dropped on you.

SOJI: She's…?

SOLA makes the shape of a pregnant woman.

Yeah, well, um, I was saying… We should start thinking, um, thinking of what kind of country we want…

SOLA: You're no longer a student union leader. The soldiers are back in their barracks. Job done.

SOJI: Seems like things are even worse.

SOLA: How would you know? Look, Nigeria doesn't need you anymore.

SOJI: I thought you liked that part of me. The mother part.

SOLA: I want it for myself.

YINKA enters from upstairs and exits to kitchen. He has a hangover. SOLA smiles as she bows her head. YINKA enters with a cup of coffee and goes upstairs.

My father my father my father…

YINKA: (*Stops, turns round.*) Excuse me?

SOJI: We were just talking –

YINKA: My brother can't see you for the trash that you are.

SOLA: It's you who's blind. Looking down your nose at everyone.

YINKA: (*To SOJI.*) You see how this thing shows me no respect?

SOLA: You want me to fear you. Who does that remind me of? Oh yeah, my father my father my father. 'Sola has no respect, Sola has no discipline. I caned her, she didn't cry. She has no remorse. I will beat you until you bleed.' You want to see the scars?

YINKA: Oh great. Another strip-show.

SOLA: You'd love that. It would remind you again of what you couldn't keep. Dear Daddy must have the beautiful house-girl for himself. Junior should go find another plaything.

YINKA: Dad did me a favour. I'd hate to have had you for a daughter.

SOLA: It's your sons I'm sorry for.

YINKA: You'll never be a true Adeyemi.

SOLA: Like I care?

YINKA: You're a pig in a house of diamonds. No name, no future.

SOLA: Brother Soji is taking me to London. I'll get away from this God-forsaken family for good.

YINKA: Which London? The same London with the Queen and Buckingham Palace? (*To SOJI.*) Please let me tell her. Please.

SOLA: You hate seeing me happy. You just have to try and –

SOJI: The university is reviewing my position. Funding's been cut. My department did poorly in the research assessment. I was one of those whose research work was deemed inadequate.

SOLA: It doesn't matter. You can return to your former college.

SOJI: Never. People were being promoted over me.

SOLA: No problem. Find another job –

YINKA: I'll put you out of your misery! He's not going back. He's got a job here.

SOLA: Rubbish. Lies.

YINKA: There's the horse's mouth.

SOLA: You led me on!

SOJI: I didn't know how to tell you.

SOLA: I made plans!

SOJI: You can always go by yourself –

SOLA slaps him and storms upstairs.

YINKA: Man, you two are not married. You can slap her back. That will wake you up. What's this rubbish about taking her to London?

SOJI: None of your business. (*Heads for front door.*)

YINKA: Come here! Don't let me call you again...

SOJI returns. YINKA hugs him.

Why didn't you tell me about your work problems? Ah, it doesn't matter. This other job should be a sure banker. Return to London and pack your things. We'll be together again. Enim's sister was sizing you up at the funeral. It's about time we made Dad more grandchildren. Abasina!

ABASINA: (*Enters from kitchen.*) Sah!

YINKA: My breakfast.

ABASINA curtseys and enters kitchen.

SOJI: For how long have you been sleeping with Abasina?

YINKA: None of your business.

SOJI: It's my business if she's –

AFOLABI enters from kitchen.

AFOLABI: Sah, I am wait for you this morning.

HELEN and PAKIMI enter. AFOLABI exits quickly.

HELEN: Morning, oh. Up so early?

YINKA exits upstairs.

SOJI: Morning. You're out and about early.

HELEN: You won't believe it. I went to the church not knowing Pastor was here already.

SOJI: Surveying your property, I see.

HELEN: Oh, you've agreed to sell Pastor some of the land. That's very kind of you. At least part of the estate will remain a part of us. Even better – it will be used to God's greater glory.

SOJI: You haven't told her? (*Laughs, rubs his cheek.*) This is a day for turning the other cheek. (*Exits upstairs.*)

PAKIMI: I wanted to tell you.

HELEN: They've told you the person they're selling the estate to. Who is it?

PAKIMI looks down.

Be serious... I don't believe it.

PAKIMI: What can I say?

HELEN: You should have told me!

PAKIMI: I tried but do you ever listen when you get agitated?

HELEN: When –

PAKIMI: We're sorting out the paperwork this evening.

HELEN: The driver is in the driving seat. (*Heads for upstairs.*)

PAKIMI: (*Holds her.*) Stay as long as you like. You know that I would never throw you out.

HELEN: They've won. They've used you to make me the harlot.

PAKIMI: Nobody's won. You'll get the settlement you deserve, I'll make sure. You are Chief Mrs Helen Adeyemi. No one can take that away from you... It's funny. We both used to dream: what would it be like to be lord and lady of the estate. I never thought we'd have to take it in turns. (*Looks up at the chandelier.*)

HELEN: About your offer –

PAKIMI: Mrs Pakimi will want to redecorate.

HELEN: Oh, of course –

PAKIMI: You said?

HELEN: Nothing. The car was making a funny noise... (*Heads to kitchen.*)

PAKIMI: Let Abasina tell Ekong to see to it...

HELEN: I have to show him. (*Exits.*)

SOLA enters from upstairs with her bags.

PAKIMI: You're leaving us? The Thanksgiving...

SOLA: I'm behind in my coursework.

PAKIMI: Okay, erm. We haven't had the chance to talk. How are you?

SOLA: Fine.

PAKIMI: It can't be fine if you're not attending your own father's Thanksgiving.

SOLA: I really don't have the time to talk.

PAKIMI: There's something wrong with the car. Let me drop you off.

SOLA: I think you have more things to worry about.

PAKIMI: It's you I'm more worried about. I don't want this to spoil our relationship. Whatever happens, you will not suffer.

SOLA: I don't get you.

PAKIMI: Oh. You haven't heard. I'll tell you on our way...

AFOLABI enters from kitchen. Retreats. PAKIMI clocks him.

AFOLABI: Sah.

PAKIMI: (*To SOLA.*) I'll meet you in the car. (*Ushers AFOLABI into kitchen.*)

SOLA looks around the house briefly then heads for the front door. SOJI enters from upstairs.

SOJI: Sola...

SOLA: Save your breath.

SOJI: What are you going to do now?

SOLA: What does it matter to you?

SOJI: I do care about you.

SOLA: I've learned to cope with disappointment all my life. I honestly thought you'd be different. What happened to you?

We all thought you'd be the next Fela, shouting from the rooftops against injustice.

SOJI: That man you wanted to have all to yourself?

SOLA: You're not that man anymore.

SOJI: I can be that man again, shouting from the rooftops.

SOLA: Let's stop fooling around. We were foolish to think that we could work out. I am getting on with my life.

SOJI: So you're going to your standby.

SOLA: I know where I stand with Wale. He wants what I want.

SOJI: He's taking you to London?

SOLA: We'll make a life here. If London comes up in future –

SOJI: Give me the chance. Stay. I'll return to London. I'll get another job.

SOLA: Move on, Soji.

PAKIMI enters.

PAKIMI: Sorry for keeping you. Brother Soji… (*Exits through front door.*)

SOJI holds SOLA. SOLA releases herself from his grip and exits. SOJI is downcast. EKONG enters through kitchen.

EKONG: Sorry, Sah. I'm looking for Abasina.

SOJI: I don't know where she is.

ABASINA enters from kitchen with washing.

Oh, there you go.

ABASINA: You dey find me, Sah?

SOJI: No, no. It's Ekong. If anyone looks for me I've gone round the estate. (*Exits through front door.*)

ABASINA: Yes, Sah.

EKONG: How the fallen are mighty, I mean, how the mighty are fallen.

ABASINA: Dem still dey inside house, oh.

EKONG: Pastor don serve Afolabi notice. He dey do (*Mimics crying.*) for backyard. I no tell am? All his years wasted. To help the rich get richer. But Abasina, money dey inside this church business, oh. I know how to pray for people. *Oya*, kneel down.

ABASINA: Mr Ekong. Everything to you is joke.

EKONG: What can I do? Pastor dey look for me too. How your stomach? No more morning sickness?

ABASINA: I no get morning sickness.

EKONG: My wife have born me three children, including the one who resemble my next door neighbour. So. You play the game. You win. As one Adeyemi door close, another one open.

ABASINA: As you talk am, we have to look after ourself... So you know about me and Papa?

EKONG: (*Nods.*) You lucky say Brother Yinka resemble Papa. If the baby no resemble dem, make you take am go do plastic surgery. If you get driver and house help, no treat dem like dirty, oh.

They hug.

Abasina! You no be small girl, oh.

ABASINA: Mr Ekong. What of you?

EKONG: Madam say make I take the car to mechanic... (*He winks, exits through the front door like a king. Sings.*) 'Revolution is coming, one day-one day...'

ABASINA: (*Looks after him.*) Mr Ekong... (*She looks at Chief Adeyemi's portrait and touches it. She pats her stomach.*)

HELEN enters.

HELEN: Ah-ah. How long does it take you to put the washing away? Ehn? God knows you will soon be out of a job, then you will see. Bastard.

ABASINA quickly exits upstairs. PAKIMI and SOLA enter.

PAKIMI: That is wrong. Totally wrong.

HELEN: What is it?

PAKIMI: Sola has something very important to say to you.

HELEN: (*Sits down.*) What is it?

PAKIMI: I didn't realise she hadn't said goodbye to you. I brought her straight back.

HELEN: Sola, is this true? You see our situation yet throughout you've behaved so badly. I'm disappointed in you. I'm only trying to give you a better life. Is that my crime that you are punishing me for?

SOLA: I didn't ask you to do anything for me.

PAKIMI: Sola! Apologise to your mother.

HELEN: That is how she talks to me. Because I didn't go to university, you are too smart to take correction from me. Because I don't have high-class friends.

PAKIMI: Sola apologise.

SOLA: You wanted me to have a heart-to-heart with my mother. If you don't like it, too bad.

PAKIMI: What has come over you?

HELEN: It is only now that you are noticing this her behaviour? Because I did not want you to end up a house-girl like me, this is the thanks I get.

SOLA: Whatever.

PAKIMI: You are starting to sound like Brother Soji.

HELEN: Abi, oh. It is too late for him to be playing big brother to you. (*To PAKIMI.*) Remember Papa's 70th. He didn't even recognise her. The fool was toasting her.

SOLA: (*Testily.*) Why do you keep bringing that up?

HELEN: Because his dirty ideas are infecting you. You know *oyinbo* people. We see them on 'Jerry Springer'. That you are

brother and sister he would say after all you are not of the
same mother.

SOLA: Can I go now?

HELEN: I don't blame you. You've never known suffering. I've
been looking after you too much –

SOLA: When did you look after me? Was it when you sent me to
boarding-school? Or when you and Papa were out partying
all night and travelling around the world? Or when you
hosted parties every week?

HELEN: It is the abundance of your riches that makes you
ungrateful.

SOLA: What have I got to be grateful for? That I had money in
my pocket? Or that everyone envied me because I was the
daughter of Chief Adeyemi and his former house-girl?

HELEN: You are a child. That's why you keep looking at the past
in that manner.

SOLA: Oh and you don't?

HELEN: I did what I thought was right –

SOLA: Because now Papa is dead and the estate is gone the
society invites will dry up.

HELEN: I was protecting you.

SOLA: You were protecting your lifestyle. You left me behind!
All because of him! (*Points at Chief Adeyemi's portrait.*)

HELEN: Sola!

SOLA: I will never be like you. I don't need any man to make
me somebody. Imagine, getting pregnant to steal him from
his wife –

*HELEN jumps up, grabs her shoe. At the same time she grabs SOLA
by the neck and beats her over the head with it.*

PAKIMI: Helen!

HELEN: (*As she hits SOLA.*) How dare you! I suffered for both of
us! If I had not pushed Chief into marrying me you would

have become a house-girl yourself! I sacrificed everything for you. Everything!

PAKIMI: Helen! (*Wrestles HELEN off SOLA.*)

HELEN: I will kill you and kill myself! You ungrateful child. If you want to go, go! Get out! (*Throws her shoe at her.*) Don't come back here if you know what is good for you! (*Storms back upstairs.*)

SOLA calmly takes her bag and exits through front door.

Evening.

YINKA and PAKIMI are sitting on the sofa, passing documents between them. SOJI and HELEN sit watching the proceedings. Enter ABASINA with a tray of drinks, which she serves to everyone.

HELEN: You're sure Ekong did not tell you where he went?

ABASINA: I no see am since the time he go mechanic, Ma.

PAKIMI: The Lord's work is done.

YINKA: (*Reads the document.*) The Lord is generous. (*Passes it to HELEN.*)

PAKIMI: (*Looks around, as if he is seeing the place for the first time.*) Indeed.

HELEN: (*Reads the document and signs.*) I will phone the mechanic.

HELEN passes the document to YINKA, who puts it in his briefcase and stands up.

SOJI: You can phone later. One last drink?

YINKA: What for?

SOJI: Just try and play happy family. Sit.

YINKA: (*Sits.*) One drink.

HELEN: The future brings the unknown but our Saviour guides us. To the Lord.

They knock glasses and drink. ABASINA enters kitchen.

SOJI: To the unknown… Sola?

HELEN: I said sorry to her. She refused to come back.

YINKA: (*Drinks up. Stands.*) Afolabi is coming with me. He should be good for another year. Soji…

SOJI: I'm spending a few days with Enim. I'll phone you when I'm ready to come over.

YINKA: Suit yourself.

HELEN: So when are we seeing Joyce and the boys?

PAKIMI: Oh yes. I learn that you want to return home permanently. That is wonderful news.

YINKA: Once I've sorted out the house and the business. I need Abasina to clean my house.

HELEN: She can't stay too long. I need her to help me pack.

YINKA exits to kitchen.

SOJI: So, Pastor. What are you going to do with the house? Tear it down?

YINKA enters from kitchen. Takes the portrait of Chief Adeyemi. HELEN wants to protest. PAKIMI gestures to her not to.

YINKA: (*To SOJI.*) Bring the other one when you're coming. (*Exits through front door.*)

PAKIMI: Tear down? God forbid. I will use it for the Pastor's quarters. Once the surveyor does his job, I'll know where to build the church.

SOJI: So the mansion has become quarters. Wow.

PAKIMI: Of course I did not mean to belittle the mansion. Keeping it will be in remembrance of Papa. You are always welcome to visit.

HELEN: When is your friend coming to pick you?

SOJI: Soon. So –

HELEN: Abasina!

ABASINA: (*Runs out.*) Ma!

HELEN: Get Brother Soji's bags from the bedroom.

ABASINA exits upstairs. She returns with the suitcases and exits through kitchen.

SOJI: So, you're now the proud owner of my father's house.

PAKIMI: The way of the world.

SOJI: Take care of the place. (*Points to the chandelier.*)

PAKIMI: First thing to do is to redecorate the interior...with your permission.

SOJI: You'll make a great diplomat, Pastor.

The sound of a car driving up the driveway. A horn honks.

That'll be Enim.

SOJI approaches PAKIMI. They shake hands.

PAKIMI: The Lord is patient. He waits for you with open arms.

SOJI: Better than Ogun waiting for me with an axe, eh? Say bye-bye to Sola for me... Tell her... Never mind. The Adeyemis have left the building! (*Exits.*)

PAKIMI: (*Looks after SOJI.*) You...

HELEN: Well.

PAKIMI: Well.

HELEN: Look after this house well, oh.

PAKIMI: Will you be all right?

HELEN: You know me.

PAKIMI: If you and Sola ever need anything. Anything...

HELEN: I will need a stick to break Ekong's head when he returns...

PAKIMI: But seriously...

HELEN: Eh, I'm fine. Papa was careless with his cheque-book. And a sensible second wife always saves for a rainy day.

PAKIMI: Nigerians, Nigerians...

HELEN: What? You took my house. Did I complain?

SOLA enters. There is a plaster on her face.

PAKIMI: The prodigal returns!

HELEN: Did you think they'd be waiting for you?

SOLA: Soji's gone?

PAKIMI: To his friend's.

A car horn.

HELEN: Tell Wale to come inside.

SOLA: We have to get back to campus. Where are you staying?

HELEN: I'll phone you when I've decided.

SOLA exits.

PAKIMI: That your daughter is as strong as anything.

HELEN: You're telling me? I need prayers on some matters.
(*Goes up the stairs.*)

PAKIMI hesitates. HELEN turns round at the middle of the stairs. She holds out her arms. PAKIMI smiles. They hold each other as they exit upstairs. Enter ABASINA from kitchen with her suitcase. She goes to the staircase to see if the coast is clear. She picks up the phone.

ABASINA: (*Whispers.*) Taxi? Ikoyi... Number 1 Adeyemi Close... Ten minutes. (*Takes the portrait of Chief and Mrs Adeyemi. Exits quietly through the kitchen.*)

Enter SOLA, crestfallen. She heads for the stairs. Enter SOJI behind her. She turns round. They look at each other.

Finish.

ALSO AVAILABLE FROM OBERON BOOKS

MARY STUART
BY SCHILLER, IN A NEW VERSION BY PETER OSWALD
ISBN 1 84002 579 4 £8.99

AS YOU DESIRE ME
BY PIRANDELLO, IN A NEW VERSION BY HUGH WHITEMORE
ISBN 1 84002 584 0 £8.99

THE HYPOCHONDRIAC
BY MOLIERE, IN A NEW VERSION BY RICHARD BEAN
ISBN 1 84002 617 0 £8.99

THE GOVERNMENT INSPECTOR
BY GOGOL, TRANSLATED AND ADAPTED BY ALISTAIR BEATON
ISBN 1 84002 583 2 £7.99

NIGHTS AT THE CIRCUS
KNEEHIGH THEATRE, ADAPTED FROM THE NOVEL BY ANGELA CARTER
ISBN 1 84002 631 6 £8.99

TRISTAN & YSEULT
THE BACCHAE / THE WOODEN FROCK / THE RED SHOES
KNEEHIGH THEATRE   ISBN 1 84002 564 6 £9.99

WOYZECK
BY BUCHNER, ADAPTED BY GISLI ORN GARDARSSON
WITH SONGS BY NICK CAVE   ISBN 1 84002 641 3 £7.99

PROFESSOR BERNHARDI
BY SCHNITZLER, TRANSLATED BY SAMUEL ADAMSON
ISBN 1 84002 552 2 £8.99

MUSIK
BY WEDEKIND, TRANSLATED BY NEIL FLEMING
ISBN 1 84002 550 6 £8.99

ROSE BERND
BY HAUPTMANN, TRANSLATED BY DENNIS KELLY
ISBN 1 84002 551 4 £8.99

THREE SISTERS
AFTER CHECKHOV, BY MUSTAPHA MATURA
ISBN 1 84002 643 X £8.99

available from all good bookshops or at www.oberonbooks.com
info@oberonbooks.com • 020 7607 3637

For information on these and other plays and books published by Oberon,
or for a free catalogue, listing all titles and cast breakdowns,
visit our website

www.oberonbooks.com

info@oberonbooks.com • 020 7607 3637